UNCIVIL WARS

UNCIVIL WARS

THE CONTROVERSY
OVER REPARATIONS
FOR SLAVERY

DAVID HOROWITZ

ENCOUNTER BOOKS
SAN FRANCISCO, CALIFORNIA

First edition published in 2002 by Encounter Books, an activity of Encounter for Culture and Education, Inc., a nonprofit tax exempt corporation.

Encounter Books website address: www.encounterbooks.com

Manufactured in the United States and printed on acid-free paper.

The paper used in this publication meets the minimum requirements of ANSI/NISO Z39.48-1992 (R 1997)(Permanence of Paper).

FIRST EDITION

Library of Congress Cataloging-in-Publication Data

Horowitz, David, 1939–
   Uncivil wars : the controversy over reparations for slavery / David Horowitz.
   p. cm.
  Includes index.
  ISBN 1-893554-44-9 (alk. paper)
1. African Americans—Claims. 2. Compensation (Law)—United States. 3. Slavery—Law and legislation—United States—History. 4. Racism—Political aspects—United States. 5. Freedom of speech—United States. 6. Political correctness—United States. 7. Education, Higher—Political aspects—United States. 8. University of California, Berkeley. 9. University of Wisconsin—Madison. 10. Brown University. I. Title.
E185.8.H83 2001
323.1'196073—dc21
                                      2001040833

10 9 8 7 6 5 4 3 2 1

To Thomas Sowell, Walter Williams, Shelby Steele, and Ward Connerly, whose insight and courage showed the way;

To the brave young college journalists who stood up to the totalitarians and won;

And to Peter Collier, whose idea and friendship made this book possible.

CONTENTS

Anyone who actually reads David Horowitz's carefully reasoned and factually-based ad will understand why his critics did not simply reply to him and try to prove him wrong.... The painful irony is that those who are crying out against the slavery of the past include many who are trying to impose an enslavement of the mind through storm-trooper tactics.

—Thomas Sowell, "Storm-troopers vs. Free Speech"

For two centuries, the very important people who managed the affairs of this society could not believe in the importance of ideas—until one day they were shocked to discover that their children, having been captured and shaped by certain ideas, were either rebelling against their authority or seceding from their society. The truth is that ideas are all important. The massive and seemingly solid institutions of any society—the economic institutions, the political institutions, the religious institutions—are always at the mercy of the ideas in the heads of the people who populate these institutions. The leverage of ideas is so immense that a slight change in the intellectual climate can and will—perhaps slowly but nevertheless inexorably—twist a familiar institution into an unrecognizable shape.

—Irving Kristol, "On Capitalism and Democracy"

THE FAULT LINE

ome might regard this book as an act of literary masochism. In the spring of 2001, I attempted to place an ad in college newspapers opposing the idea of paying reparations for slavery 136 years after the fact. In my view the idea of reparations was self-defeating for the descendants of slaves, and divisive for everyone else. Already a drumbeat of backing for reparations had begun at the level of municipal and even state governments around the nation. The issue seemed an important one to discuss publicly before it attained a critical mass in legislative assemblies. Moreover, it intersected with an ongoing national "dialogue on race" which, since the very origins of this country, has been the most important dialogue Americans can have.

But when my ad appeared on college campuses, the reactions were volcanic and the attacks on me were savage. On campus after campus, protests erupted and indiscriminate rage spilled over into every corner of the public space. It was a breathtaking display of intolerance for an academic community. In their anger, my critics showed little regard for fairness or facts, or common decency. Although I have a long public history as an activist for civil rights, I was attacked in terms normally reserved for bigots of the political fringe. Though my opponents failed to identify a single phrase I had written that denigrated any race or group, my ad was called "hate speech," "racist" and even "Hitlerian" (this in a lengthy response to my arguments by a professor of Afro-American Studies and the editor of the *Black Scholar*).[1]

Fortunately, I had my defenders, like Jonathan Yardley of the *Washington Post,* who described the attacks as "hogwash." He was joined by John Leo of *U.S. News & World Report* and by the distinguished black scholar Thomas Sowell, along with the editors of *USA Today,* the *Boston Globe,* the *Philadelphia Inquirer* and other papers, who understood the difference between honest disagreement over ideas and hate. Even the liberal columnist Richard Cohen wrote in the *Washington Post,* "there's not a lot in Horowitz's ad with which I disagree."[2]

My opponents' agenda in this controversy was not to refute the ideas the ad contained, but to obliterate the individual who was responsible for them. This had been a classic tactic of twentieth-century totalitarians. In Stalin's Soviet Union, for example, the charge against all dissidents, whatever their views, was that they were "anti-Soviets" and "enemies of the people." This isolated them from the world of common decency and created grounds for their "liquidation." No such drastic measures were imagined here. But there was a clear agenda to identify me—and college editors who printed the ad—with ideas and positions so repellent that any community of right-thinking people would reject us.

In order to describe the events that took place and even attempt to decipher their meaning, I have been forced to chronicle the details of the attack against me. It has not been a pleasant experience. Who would want to endure, let alone remember, such enmity? Yet as the attacks unfolded, many of my critics in the press attempted to minimize their severity by facilely concluding that the entire episode was a political stunt I had dreamed up to win "fame and profit," as Clarence Page of the *Chicago Tribune* actually wrote. What was he thinking? Who would want to become famous as a "Nazi racist?"

The controversy put me in an unfamiliar as well as a painful position. I had marched in my first civil rights protest more than fifty years before in behalf of President Truman's Fair Employment Practices Commission, which outlawed discrimination against blacks in the civil service. I have spent much of my adult life in similar battles for black Americans whose ancestors were brought to this country in chains and whose rights have been denied more than those of any other group. Members of

---

1. Robert Chrisman and Ernest Allen Jr., "Ten Reasons: A Response to David Horowitz," www.umass.edu/afroam/hor.html.

2. Jonathan Yardley, "Politically Corrected," *Washington Post,* 5 March 2001; Richard Cohen, "Specious Speech," *Washington Post,* 22 March 2001.

my family are black and I have partly black grandchildren whose future is at stake in these issues.

In the 1970s, my efforts for civil rights led me into a deep involvement with the Black Panther Party, whom progressives, at the time, were calling the "vanguard of the black revolution." I was attracted to them especially because while other civil rights organizations of the post-King era were all words, and unpleasant words at that, the Panthers appeared to be actually helping people "on the ground" with their breakfast programs for children and health clinics; because they appeared to check the histrionic violence of black nationalist groups; and because they still preached coalitions with whites. But the Panthers turned out to be a vanguard of gangsters, some of whom killed an innocent friend of mine and derailed my life for nearly a decade.[3]

This tragedy could have caused me to become cynical and bitter, but I had invested too much in the idea that individuals should be judged on their merits, not as members of a racial group. I was the one who had been blind, and I could not escape my responsibility by blaming someone else. Under the spell of seductive ideas about "social justice," I had failed to see the character of the people I became involved with, and had linked others—also blinded—to their destructive cause. After this episode, I decided that my future efforts in behalf of racial justice would be undertaken with open eyes.

My opposition to the reparations agenda, as I will make clear in this narrative, is a product of these sobering experiences and second thoughts. It is not that I eschew "noble causes," but that I have learned to evaluate them with a skeptic's eye and to judge them first by their practical consequences. Examining the reparations movement, I came to the conclusion that it was destructive in ways similar to the radical causes I once supported, which have hurt the prospects for ever discovering a promised land that lies "beyond race."

The pursuit of justice for all individuals is still the goal that shapes my interests as a political writer and social activist, and a continuing source of my self-respect. On more than one occasion during the writing of this book, the malicious comments I was forced to record caused me to flinch. At these times, I asked myself whether I should have taken on the battle in the first place. During the controversy, one of my sons asked another member of the family, "Why would dad want to do this? Why would he

---

3. These events are narrated in my autobiography, *Radical Son: A Generational Odyssey* (New York, 1997).

want to be called a *racist?*" Indeed, why would anyone want to put his son in the position where he would have to ask such a question?

This book is an attempt to provide an answer. Although I am the author of its narrative, its subject is not me; nor is it the advertisement that provoked such a reaction. Similar events have taken place before on hundreds and maybe thousands of campuses and similar attacks have been made on hundreds and maybe thousands of individuals—professors, students and campus visitors.

In 1997, to take just one example, a tenured Texas law professor named Lino Graglia, who had taught for thirty-three years without incident, overnight became the target of the same forces I did when he made one remark that the local press quoted in garbled form and out of context. Graglia is a recognized expert on constitutional law and a longstanding public opponent of racial preferences in university admissions, and his legal opinions have been solicited by congressional bodies. When asked by a reporter to explain the low test scores of minority students, he made the commonplace observation that in some minority communities, educational achievement often did not receive support in the home. What followed was a public lynching—of Graglia's reputation. The NAACP accused him of "racial harassment," the Hispanic caucus in the Texas state legislature demanded his dismissal, fifty law professors wrote a letter condemning his remarks, and Jesse Jackson told a cheering rally of five thousand students on the University of Texas campus that Graglia should be treated as a "moral and social pariah" for his "racist, fascist, offensive speech."[4]

The difference between what happened to Lino Graglia and others like him, and what transpired when I placed an ad against reparations in a series of college papers, was that their experiences remained isolated and individual. As a result they could be seen as idiosyncratic, the product of unique circumstances. But the placing of my ad on campuses across the country was like parachuting flares into a nighttime war zone. In an eye blink, their appearance illuminated the dark places of the educational landscape, and the suppression of free speech that is now routine in the academy became national news.

America is a democracy composed of diverse cultures and ethnic communities. Our future, like our past, depends on fidelity to ideas and

---

4. Martin P. Golding, *Free Speech on Campus* (New York, 2000), p. 82. For studies corroborating Graglia's contention cf. John McWhorter, *Losing the Race: Self-Sabotage in Black America* (New York, 2000).

ideals that inspire a common identity—*e pluribus unum.* The fault line that threatens this American identity is race. What this means is that there can be no common future if America becomes unable to maintain the affections of its diverse communities or if its political divisions become defined by race.

In the 2000 presidential campaign, candidate Al Gore touched this fault line when he challenged the idea that Supreme Court justices should adhere to the meaning of the constitutional text. He said: "I often think of the strictly constructionist meaning that was applied when the Constitution was written, how some people were considered three-fifths of a human being." In making these remarks, the vice president had fallen under the spell of a revisionist message that the United States Constitution is racially suspect. It is a false history, but it has been repeated so often and over so many years that it is already ingrained as popular myth, particularly among Americans of African descent. African-American students at Duke University protesting my ad, for example, chanted, "We are not three-fifths of a student."

In fact the United States Constitution does not mention race, let alone consider Americans who are black to be three-fifths of a human being. The famous three-fifths compromise was made over the census count of *slaves.* While all slaves were black, at the time the Constitution was written there were also tens of thousands of free blacks who were citizens and whom the census counted as full human beings. The purpose of the count was to determine the assignment of congressional districts, and thus the distribution of governmental power. It was the *anti*-slavery Founders who proposed the three-fifths compromise in order to *diminish* the electoral strength of the slaveholding South. It was the party of slavery, on the other side, that wanted to count slaves as *full* citizens in order to increase their power to protect the slave system. In other words, from the point of view of the slaves themselves, it would have been better (and truer) had they been counted as only one-fifth of a citizen, or—better still—not at all. The slander against the Constitution contained in the myth about the three-fifths rule is even worse in its ramifications than the slander of individuals, because it is an assault on the very foundations of the nation.

This narrative, then, is about a dubious issue—reparations for slavery—and the fierce response that an effort to initiate a dialogue about this issue caused. In a larger sense it is also a book about the intellectual vulgarities of American universities in an age of "political correctness." It shows that the term "politically correct" is actually far too genteel a description for what is better understood as a totalitarian mind-set. It reveals, in the inner sanctums of our most elite universities, swamps of almost bottomless ignorance and malice. It makes disturbingly clear that the liberal arts divisions of American institutions of higher learning are breeding grounds of some of the most retrograde ideas and reactionary trends in our political culture and, worse, shows that the behaviors are protected and even encouraged by the guardians of the institutions themselves.

Los Angeles, July 4, 2001

THE CONTROVERSY

The Horowitz controversy has laid bare the cultural and intellectual splits that rivet the contemporary university....

—Donald Downs, Professor of Political Science, Journalism and Law at the University of Wisconsin

ONE

THE AD

T he ad I decided to place in a series of college papers in the spring of 2001 gave "Ten Reasons" why reparations for slavery was a bad idea. It was a position that 75 percent of Americans shared according to current public opinion polls.[5] An accurate parsing of its text was provided by a reporter for the *Los Angeles Times:*

> The gist of the 10 points in Horowitz's ad was that the Civil War is long over, African Americans are prospering today, and the families of most of today's Americans bear no responsibility for slavery or the Jim Crow laws that followed anyway. Why, he asked, should a struggling recent immigrant have to pay for injustices that happened in another time?[6]

The formal title of my ad was "Ten Reasons Why Reparations for Slavery Is a Bad Idea—and Racist Too,"[7] and it was eventually sent to seventy-one college papers nationwide. Forty-three of these papers rejected it outright, many conceding that their objection was to the ideas it expressed.

---

5. The polls were conducted by *Time* and Fox News.
6. Fred S. Dickey, "An Uncivil Discourse: The Uproar over David Horowitz's Ad in the UC Berkeley Newspaper Has Challenged One of the Fundamentals of University Life: the Free Exchange of Ideas," *Los Angeles Times Magazine,* 6 May 2001.
7. A select bibliography of 101 articles about the ad that appeared in national magazines and newspapers or on Internet sites, and 301 articles that appeared in state, local and college papers is available at www.frontpagemagazine.com.

In other words, the college editors who rejected the ad wanted to prevent the most educated people in America from being exposed to what it said.

When the ad was actually printed, things got even worse. There were protest demonstrations, demands for resignations of the editors and even thefts of whole press runs. This was in stark contrast to what had happened when I published the same ideas in a column for the Internet journal *Salon.com* nine months earlier. The title of the column I wrote was identical except for three words. In *Salon*, I wrote that reparations were a bad idea "for black people," a phrase I later thought might be considered presumptuous and possibly "insensitive" in the politically correct campus environment.[8] In writing the ad, I dropped the phrase to avoid provoking a reaction.

When the campuses reacted anyway, my *Salon* editor, Joan Walsh, recalled with some bewilderment the response to the original column. In an article called "Who's Afraid of the Big Bad Horowitz?" Walsh wrote: "We received hundreds of letters about the column, most but not all of them critical. We ran a rejoinder by a regular *Salon* contributor, Earl Ofari Hutchinson, supporting reparations. We got even more letters, as Horowitz supporters slammed Hutchinson. The debate was lively, arguments on all sides got thoroughly aired, and a good time was had by all. Nobody picketed our offices. Nobody came to *Salon* with a list of grievances to be addressed. Nobody sought or was given an apology. Nobody called us racist."[9]

I had written the column in response to a news report about a vote in the city of Chicago. Its council had passed a resolution favoring reparations for slavery by a margin of 46 to 1.[10] Until then, I had always regarded the reparations movement as an obscure fringe cause. The lopsided vote was a sign to me that something was changing.

In the news story, Chicago alderman Dorothy Tillman was identified as the sponsor of the council resolution. She was quoted as saying, "America owes blacks a debt because ... we built this country on free labor, and wealth was handed down to the white community." The lone "no" vote had been cast by Alderman Brian Doherty, the council's only Republican. Doherty described slavery as "a horrible crime," but said,

---

8. "Ten Reasons Why Reparations for Slavery Are a Bad Idea for Black People—And Racist Too," 30 May 2000. The *Salon* copy editors also regarded "reparations" as a plural noun, while I did not.

9. Joan Walsh, "Who's Afraid of the Big Bad Horowitz?" *Salon.com*, 9 March 2001. Earl Ofari Hutchinson, "Debt Wrong: It's Time for the United States to Pay Up for Slavery," *Salon.com*, 6 June 2000.

10. Gary Washburn, "Daley, Council Join in Slavery Apology," *Chicago Tribune*, 18 May 2000. See also Flynn McRoberts and Monica Davey, "Aldermen Back Bid for Slavery Reparations," *Chicago Tribune*, 27 April 2000.

"the constituents of [my] Northwest Side ward are, by and large, the descendants of people who immigrated to the United States after slavery had ended. They should not be forced to pay for wrongs committed by others."[11] This seemed a reasonable position, which suggested to me that the unanimous vote of Democrats on the council might be attributed to an atmosphere of intimidation that made some of them reluctant to challenge the resolution out of fear of being charged with "racism."

After the vote was taken, Mayor Richard Daley made a public apology for slavery. This also caught my attention. After all, Illinois was a free state before the Civil War. Its men had spilled their blood in this great conflict, and its present-day citizens were usually proud of their anti-slavery heritage, emblazoning their license plates with the motto "Land of Lincoln." This practice had even made them targets of segregationist attacks when they traveled to the South during the civil rights struggles of the 1950s and '60s. What had an Illinois native like Mayor Daley to apologize *for* when it came to slavery?

Such were the sentiments the Chicago vote provoked in me, as I noted in my *Salon* column. Then, nine months later, I came across an Internet notice announcing a conference on reparations at the University of Chicago. The conference was scheduled for February 9, 2001, in the middle of Black History Month.[12] A "Reparations Rally" was also scheduled for February 6 at California State University, Northridge. Other campuses were promoting "Reparations Awareness" days to mobilize support for the new cause. A feature of all these collegiate events was that only one side of the reparations argument would be represented. This was the fruit of nearly two decades of activists' efforts to make universities reflect their political agendas under the imperative of being "politically correct."

It seemed to me that one-party politics were not appropriate for academic institutions or healthy for the democracy these institutions were supposed to serve. If universities could not be counted on to support more than one side of a question, what institutions could? Such thoughts prompted a hasty decision to cut the *Salon* article to the length of a newspaper page and place it as an ad in the *Chicago Maroon* and Cal State Northridge's *Sun Dial* so that the students attending these events would be able to see another side of the issue. I included a coupon at the end of the ad, which itself became a subject of controversy:

11. Ibid.
12. A week earlier, a "National Reparations Convention" organized by Alderman Tillman also took place in Chicago. See Ruth Igoe, "Reparations Forum Ends with a Proposal," *Chicago Tribune*, 5 February 2001.

■   ■   ■   ■   ■

Ten Reasons Why
Reparations for Slavery
Is a Bad Idea—and Racist Too.

I
There Is No Single Group Responsible
for the Crime of Slavery.

Black Africans and Arabs were responsible for enslaving the ancestors of African-Americans. There were 3,000 black slave-owners in the antebellum United States. Are reparations to be paid by their descendants too? There were white slaves in colonial America. Are their descendents going to receive payments?

II
There Is No Single Group That
Benefited Exclusively from Slavery.

The claim for reparations is premised on the false assumption that only whites have benefited from slavery. If slave labor has created wealth for Americans, then obviously it has created wealth for black Americans as well, including the descendants of slaves. The GNP of black America makes the African-American community the tenth most prosperous "nation" in the world. American blacks on average enjoy per capita incomes in the range of twenty to fifty times that of blacks living in any of the African nations from which they were kidnapped.

III
Only a Minority of White Americans Owned Slaves,
While Others Gave Their Lives to Free Them.

Only a tiny minority of Americans ever owned slaves. This is true even for those who lived in the antebellum South where only one white in five was a slaveholder. Why should their descendants owe a debt? What about the descendants of the 350,000 Union soldiers who died to free the slaves? They gave their lives. What morality would ask their descendants to pay again? If paying reparations on the basis of skin color is not racism, what is?

IV
Most Living Americans Have No Connection
(Direct or Indirect) to Slavery.

The two great waves of American immigration occurred after 1880 and then after 1960. What logic would require Vietnamese boat people, Russian refuseniks, Iranian refugees, Armenian victims of the Turkish persecution, Jews, Mexicans Greeks, or Polish, Hungarian, Cambodian and Korean victims of Communism, to pay reparations to American blacks?

V
The Historical Precedents Used to Justify
the Reparations Claim Do Not Apply, and the Claim Itself
Is Based on Race Not Injury.

The historical precedents generally invoked to justify the reparations claim are payments to Jewish survivors of the Holocaust, Japanese-Americans and African-American victims of racial experiments in Tuskegee, or racial outrages in Rosewood and Oklahoma City. But in each case, the recipients of reparations were the direct victims of the injustice or their immediate families. This would be the only case of reparations to people who were not immediately affected and whose sole qualification to receive reparations would be racial. During the slavery era, many blacks were free men or slave-owners themselves, yet the reparations claimants make no attempt to take this fact into account. If this is not racism, what is?

VI
The Reparations Argument Is Based on the Unsubstantiated
Claim That All African-Americans Suffer from the Economic
Consequences of Slavery and Discrimination.

No scientific attempt has been made to prove that living individuals have been adversely affected by a slave system that was ended nearly 150 years ago. But there is plenty of evidence that the hardships of slavery were hardships that individuals could and did overcome. The black middle class in America is a prosperous community that is now larger in absolute terms than the black underclass. Its existence suggests that present economic adversity is the result of failures of individual character rather than the lingering after-effects of racial discrimination or a slave system that ceased to exist well over a century ago. West Indian blacks in America are also descended from slaves but their average incomes are equivalent to the average incomes of whites (and nearly 25 percent higher than the average incomes of American-born blacks). How is it that slavery adversely affected one large group of descendants but not the other? How can government be expected to decide an issue that is so subjective?

VII
The Reparations Claim Is One More Attempt to Turn African-Americans into Victims. It Sends a Damaging Message to the African-American Community and to Others.

The renewed sense of grievance—which is what the claim for reparations will inevitably create—is not a constructive or helpful message for black leaders to send to their communities and to others. To focus the social passions of African-Americans on what some other Americans may have done to their ancestors 50 or 150 years ago is to burden them with a crippling sense of victimhood. How are the millions of non-black refugees from tyranny and genocide who are now living in America going to receive these claims, moreover, except as demands for special treatment—an extravagant new handout that is only necessary because some blacks can't seem to locate the ladder of opportunity within reach of others, many of whom are less privileged than themselves?

VIII
Reparations to African-Americans Have Already Been Paid.

Since the passage of the Civil Rights Acts and the advent of the Great Society in 1965, trillions of dollars in transfer payments have been made to African-Americans in the form of welfare benefits and racial preferences (in contracts, job placements and educational admissions)—all under the rationale of redressing historic racial grievances. It is said that reparations are necessary to achieve a healing between African-Americans and other Americans. If trillion-dollar restitutions and a wholesale rewriting of American law (in order to accommodate racial preferences) is not enough to achieve a "healing," what is?

IX
What about the Debt Blacks Owe to America?

Slavery existed for thousands of years before the Atlantic slave trade, and in all societies. But in the thousand years of slavery's existence, there never was an anti-slavery movement until white Anglo-Saxon Christians created one. If not for the anti-slavery beliefs and military power of white Englishmen and Americans, the slave trade would not have been brought to an end. If not for the sacrifices of white soldiers and a white American president who gave his life to sign the Emancipation Proclamation, blacks in America would still be slaves. If not for the dedication of Americans of all ethnicities and colors to a society based on the principle that all men are created equal, blacks in America would not enjoy the highest standard of living of blacks anywhere in the world, and indeed one of the highest standards of living of any people in the world. They would not enjoy the greatest freedoms and the most thoroughly protected individual rights anywhere. Where is the acknowledgment of black America and its leaders for those gifts?

X
The Reparations Claim Is a Separatist Idea That Sets African-Americans against the Nation That Gave Them Freedom.

Blacks were here before the Mayflower. Who is more American than the descendants of African slaves? For the African-American community to isolate itself from America is to embark on a course whose implications are troubling. Yet the African-American community has had a long-running flirtation with separatists, nationalists and the political left, who want African-Americans to be no part of America's social contract. African-Americans should reject this temptation.

For all America's faults, African-Americans have an enormous stake in this country and its heritage. It is this heritage that is really under attack by the reparations movement. The reparations claim is one more assault on America, conducted by racial separatists and the political left. It is an attack not only on white Americans, but on all Americans—especially African-Americans.

America's African-American citizens are the richest and most privileged black people alive, a bounty that is a direct result of the heritage that is under assault. The American idea needs the support of its African-American citizens. But African-Americans also need the support of the American idea. For it is the American idea that led to the principles and created the institutions that have set African-Americans—and all of us—free.

The *Chicago Maroon* printed the ad as written, but the *Northridge Sun Dial* said no. I decided to try placing it in ten more schools, including my *alma maters* Columbia and UC Berkeley. I hoped that an ad in the *Harvard Crimson* might provoke a debate in the backyard of Afro-American Studies Department chairman Henry Louis Gates Jr. and black law professor Charles Ogletree, who were the most prestigious academic figures lending their names and support to the reparations cause.[13]

The rejections came swiftly: American University, Penn, Columbia, Virginia, Harvard, Notre Dame and the University of Washington. If the pattern had continued, I would at least have had the satisfaction of knowing that another side of the issue had been aired in three schools, even if there was no wider result. But at two of the schools that published the ad, the editors had second thoughts. It was their reactions—and the response of one editor at Berkeley in particular—that triggered the events that followed.

13. I wrote a letter to Gates on March 8, 2001, proposing a debate, but he never replied. "A Challenge to Harvard," www.frontpagemagazine.com.

No demand for "dialogue" existed prior to
your effort to provoke it.
—Assistant Chancellor John Cummins,
in a letter, March 12, 2001

TWO

THE ADMINISTRATORS (BERKELEY)

U C Berkeley is more than a university; it is a symbol. In the 1950s, it was the site of an infamous loyalty oath and became the academic institution most famously damaged by the excesses of the McCarthy era. When the state of California required the oath of faculty members to weed out suspected Communists, some of Berkeley's most prestigious scientific researchers chose to relocate rather than sign. Many went to Berkeley's rival, Stanford, a private institution that did not require political litmus tests for its scholars. In the 1960s, a reverse trend took hold and Berkeley became the symbol of a student rebellion that rocked academic institutions across the nation, beginning the long march of campus radicals to academic seats of power from which they have since politicized university life.

I had been present at the creation, so to speak, arriving in Berkeley in the summer of 1959 as a young graduate student. Working with radicals I met there, I helped to create a magazine called *Root and Branch*, one of the first publications of the New Left. In 1962, we also organized the first significant campus demonstration against the Vietnam War, the forerunner of others that would eventually reach from one end of the country to the other and polarize a generation.

In the events following the publication of my reparations ad, Berkeley now resumed its symbolic function as an indicator of political trends. The story that follows is told in detail because it provides a case study in how the politically correct university, which we criticize and joke about from without, actually works its malice from within. In the contours of these episodes at universities both public and private one can see the outlines of a malaise that has overtaken American higher learning, and shows no signs of abating.

As a result of Berkeley's status as a political weather vane, the media were paying special attention to events unfolding around the campus paper, the *Daily Californian,* when my ad appeared on Wednesday, February 28, 2001. Within hours, forty angry black students accompanied by their political mentor, a professor of African-American studies, invaded the paper's editorial offices in Eshelman Hall. In a raucous finger-wagging session, they accused editor in chief Daniel Hernandez of running an ad that was "racist" and "incorrect," and demanded a printed apology. To put Hernandez even more on the defensive, they told him that as a member of an "oppressed" (Hispanic) group he should have known better, and demanded an end to "institutional racism" at his paper. Then, with Hernandez looking on, they tore up copies of the issue containing the ad that were lying around the office.[14]

When the next issue appeared on the following day, it contained a statement by the editors regretting that they had "allowed the *Daily Cal* to become an inadvertent vehicle for bigotry." The statement was accompanied by a *mea culpa* from Hernandez himself:

> Yesterday's edition of *The Daily Californian* managed to anger more readers than anything the newspaper has printed in years. The newspaper printed an advertisement promoting a book by declaring that reparations for slavery is wrong and racist. Printed with terrible irony on the last day of Black History Month, the ad essentially said that the black community should not complain about slavery.[15]

In getting almost everything possible wrong about the facts, Hernandez's statement was typical of what was to come. To begin with, the ad did not promote a book. Secondly, it was not an ad saying that "the black community should not complain about slavery," as Hernandez wrote, or that "slavery was self-inflicted by blacks," as the *Daily Cal* "reported" in its front-page story.[16] Such ideas were too absurd for anyone to entertain. In fact, the "Ten Reasons" of the ad were not even an argument

---

14. Fred Dickey, "An Uncivil Discourse"; Daniel Hernandez, "The Ad, the Apology, and the Aftermath," *Cal Monthly,* June 2001.

15. "Letter from the Editor: Holding Ourselves Accountable," *Daily Californian,* 1 March 2001.

16. *Daily Californian,* 2 March 2001.

against reparations for slavery, but against the idea that reparations should be paid to people who were not and had never been slaves.

If, as Hernandez claimed, there was an irony hidden in the fact that the ad appeared during Black History Month, that was because reparations advocates had chosen Black History Month to stage their events. Even if this were not the case, why describe the irony as "terrible"? Is there only one attitude towards reparations that can be called "black"?

It was a lot of mistakes for only two sentences, particularly since these sentences contained *all* that Hernandez had to say about the actual contents of the ad. Almost everything that followed was an attempt to wriggle out of responsibility for running it by explaining that the paper's editorial and advertising departments were separate, and that "an admitted and terribly consequential series of missteps and miscommunications" had led to his ignorance of what the advertising department had approved. "I promise readers, it will never happen again," he wrote.

In what was to become a common theme among editors who rejected the ad, Hernandez purported to see a difference between free speech in the editorial pages and in the advertising section. "Buying space to preach a viewpoint is unfair in that it does not allow an opposing view to directly answer." This was nonsense, of course. First, because paid speech is also speech, and second, because Hernandez himself could have taken the entire paper to answer my ad had he wanted. In fact, a response to the "ten reasons" never did appear in Hernandez's paper or almost any other paper among the more than seventy to which the ad was submitted.[17]

Approaching the end of his apology, Hernandez defended himself against his radical accusers. "Let it be clear: there is no institutional racism running rampant at the *Daily Cal*." Then he reiterated his pledge: "Making sure this never happens again will now become my foremost project as I finish this semester as editor." In a later interview with the *Los Angeles Times*, Hernandez was unnervingly candid about his rationale for censorship: "I think people are too quick to dismiss political correctness.... Latino and African-American students whose ancestors [were persecuted] are now in a position to say, 'We don't have to listen to that.' This is a reversal of fortune, a reversal of suppression."[18]

The idea of reversing "suppression," however inchoate it may sound, was actually more or less the message of a famous pronouncement made

17. The three that I am aware of are the student papers at Stanford, Duke, and UC Santa Barbara. The Duke response was written by historian John Hope Franklin and is discussed below, pp. 79–83. The Santa Barbara response was written by a student and is discussed on p. 74 below.
18. Fred Dickey, "An Uncivil Discourse."

in the 1960s by Herbert Marcuse, a New Left professor at the University of California (San Diego) and a seminal influence on the tenured radicals who later created the educational curriculum for students like Daniel Hernandez. In a celebrated essay, Marcuse claimed that American democracy was in effect a sham. It represented the rule of a "repressive tolerance" that allowed anti-leftist ideas to flourish and caused radical ideas to wither on the vine. "Free speech" was the privilege of a capitalist ruling class who could buy the means of communication. To radicals seeking to overthrow the "system," Marcuse recommended a policy of intolerance, which he (dialectally) called "liberating *tolerance*" but which entailed suppressing the ideas the left opposed. "Liberating tolerance," Marcuse wrote, "would mean intolerance against movements from the Right, and toleration of movements from the Left."[19] It was an Orwellian formula that student radicals have found irresistible.

Hernandez's self-abasing *mea culpa* failed to appease the radicals, however. To them, it seemed "more like a list of excuses and procedures that should have been followed instead of an apology." The left made its displeasure clear in a flier it distributed on campus: "The refusal of the *Daily Cal* to run a full front-page apology for the racist ad placed by David Horowitz is a mode of silent support."[20]

As a result of Hernandez's capitulation, the *Daily Cal* offices were flooded with a thousand e-mails, most of them criticizing him or his politically correct surrender to the activists. But the criticisms that must have stung most came from the profession it was his ambition to join. The industry trade paper, *Editor and Publisher,* excoriated his editorial as "*mea maxima culpa* overdrive" and singled out his attack on advocacy ads: "Of course, if the *Daily Cal* won't even sell Horowitz space to argue against reparations for North American slavery, it's pretty clear that this viewpoint is taboo on opinion pages as well." Hernandez was accused of "compromising" the First Amendment, and hypocrisy: "The *Daily Cal* had no criticism at all for the protesters who ended a meeting with editors by demonstrating their own idea of free speech: They removed all remaining copies of the paper from the racks around campus."[21]

Northeast of Berkeley, at UC Davis, the editors of the *California Aggie* had taken a parallel tack, giving the media an even bigger story. The ad in the *Aggie* had apparently also bypassed the editorial process. After the furor had begun, editor Eleeza Agopian formally apologized, calling

19. Herbert Marcuse and Robert Paul Wolff, *A Critique of Pure Tolerance* (Boston, 1969), p. 109.
20. "Daily Cal Issues Apology over Controversial Ad," *Daily Californian,* 2 March 2001.
21. Mark Fitzgerald, "Murdering the First," *Editor and Publisher,* 12 March 2001.

the publication of the ad a "grievous mistake" and "an embarrassment not only for the newspaper, but the university community at large." The appearance of the ad, she wrote, had made the paper a "vehicle for racism." It was a threat to "an open and welcoming environment" as called for in UC Davis's "Principles of Community."[22]

By this time, press coverage of the growing controversy already included stories in the *San Francisco Chronicle*, the *Oakland Tribune*, the *San Jose Mercury-News*, the *Contra Costa Times*, the *Davis Enterprise*, the *Los Angeles Times* and local television news. It was on the AP wires and in national press like the *Wall Street Journal* and the *New York Daily News*, which ran a column by John Leo, called "The New Censors," reflecting the thrust of the general coverage. It was also rapidly spreading over the web at *FoxNews.com, DiversityInc.com, Newsmax.com, Poynter.org, NationalReviewOnline* and other familiar sites.

In the *Washington Post*, Jonathan Yardley derided the "keening and breast-beating" at Berkeley and Davis. "Horowitz's case isn't ironclad, and staying true to character, he makes it with in-your-face pugnacity," he wrote, but added: "he is within the grounds of fair political debate."

> Crying racism or any other ism—sexism, ageism, imperialism, homophobia, you name it—is the easy way out. Instead of coming to grips with the case made by one's opponents, just smear them with the tar of bigotry.... It's an old trick that's been employed by just about every special interest group in today's hothouse of competing grievances, and by now most Americans probably are wise to it. But the American college campus is a foreign country; they do things differently there.[23]

At the end of the week, *USA Today* provided the first of several strongly worded editorials in defense of free expression which would appear in the national press, and eventually include the *Boston Globe*, the *Chicago Tribune*, the *Arizona Republic* and the *Philadelphia Inquirer*: "Who said college campuses are the perfect spot for encouraging the open exchange of differing ideas? Certainly not some of the student newspapers that serve them. In fact, judged by their recent actions, the student papers at the University of California at Berkeley and at Davis intend to flee from free speech."[24]

---

22. "*The California Aggie* Apologizes for Running Horowitz Ad," *California Aggie*, 2 March 2001.

23. Jonathan Yardley, "Politically Corrected," *Washington Post*, 5 March 2001.

24. *USA Today*, 8 March 2001.

In fact, there was no real possibility of fleeing free speech in the age of the Internet. The "Ten Reasons" were posted on my website at www.frontpagemagazine.com, and many others replicated it. Even though Hernandez would have preferred to deny his readership the benefit of the discussion, the tremendous pressure in favor of an open exchange prompted him to devote two issues to letters to the editor and to balance them on both sides:

Anti-

> *I am appalled that the* Daily Californian *would print a full-page ad so racist and inflammatory. Although the* Daily Cal *has offered an apology, I cannot accept it! There are no words that can accommodate your act, nor the holocaust of enslavement. The negative impact of slavery is still present in America. How could the* Daily Cal *allow David Horowitz to promote racist propaganda—all for $1200 in advertisement revenue....*
>
> Charri Hearn, UC Berkeley alumnus

> *I know there's free speech and all that, but to have taken money for an ad like that and printed it in our newspaper? What does that say about our prestigious university, which already is going under scrutiny for being unwelcoming and unfair to minorities?*
>
> Sunny Horn, UC Berkeley student

> *David Horowitz's proclamation that U.S. slavery was basically self-inflicted and therefore absolves white America of any responsibility is malevolent to such an extreme that even money-grabbing functionaries on the* Daily Cal's *advertising side should have had enough sense to throw up a huge red flag. In my view, though, this guy for the right amount of cash would fabricate "research" declaring, for example, the Holocaust a hoax and the massive slaughter of American Indians a historical lie.*
>
> Jerry Holl, Berkeley resident

> *I am extremely upset, offended and appalled by the complete disregard of the black community on this campus by the* Daily Cal *staff, specifically the editing staff. The racist ad published on February 28 was a slap in the face to the hundreds of thousands of blacks who lost their lives during slavery, reconstruction, the civil rights movement, and to those who continue to be the victims of white aggression and intolerance.*
>
> Ambi Bohannon, UC Berkeley student

> *I am thoroughly offended, disgusted, and outraged that David Horowitz's ad "essentially slipped through the cracks." ... Never again should an ad be published in a paper that is connected to such*

an institution of high statutes where students of all ethnic backgrounds study to earn degrees.

Kenya Bingham, UC Berkeley student

Pro-

The Daily Cal'*s response to David Horowitz's ad is outrageous.... The normal means used to object to content found in a newspaper is to craft a letter to the editor stating one's views, rather than to react violently and make demands like a common extortionist.... If all the content that people may potentially disagree with is removed, there will be no ads, no news stories or anything at all in print.*

Linda-Kay Dolan, UC Berkeley alumnus

As a UC Berkeley graduate, I'm embarrassed and dispirited. Whatever happened to brave Daily Cal *editors who had the* cojones *to proudly buck the establishment? And make no mistake; the establishment today is leftist political correctness.*

Carl Moore, UC Berkeley alumnus

Why should the presence of 20 angry students in Eshelman Hall cause the Daily Cal *to issue a front-page apology? Twenty students could be rounded up to protest sex on Tuesday.... The* Daily Cal *has sent a clear message that they will censor themselves at the whim of the smallest of minorities.*

Jeffrey Holman, UC Berkeley student

The Daily Cal *may not think that advertisements are "free speech," but the U.S. Supreme Court clearly does. In the landmark 1964 case* New York Times v. Sullivan, *the court flatly rejected the argument that advertisements about controversial political subjects deserve less protection than other forms of speech.*

Ben Sheffner, UC Berkeley alumnus

In today's culture, "racism" is a loaded word, and can't be easily disproved or taken back. Consequently anybody should take great care and thought before calling someone a bigot. This is doubly true of someone who is supposed to be a journalist. Freedom of the press does not grant permission to commit slander. In its apology, the Daily Cal *has painted everyone who generally agrees with Horowitz's opinions as being a bigot. When do those people get an apology?*

Tim Thompson, Bryant, Arkansas

Not only was it impossible to suppress ideas on one politically correct campus, others were now erupting. Four days after Hernandez's apology, the University of Wisconsin's *Badger Herald* printed the ad, prompting a mob of 150 student protesters to besiege its offices and demand the resignation of its editor. At Brown enraged students stole an entire issue of the offending campus paper declaring it "a newspaper run by Brown-student opportunists and careerists who are completely unaccountable to the University's aims and its student body."[25] These two incidents turned what was already a contentious issue into a *cause célèbre*.

■   ■

Despite the ruckus that the ad had caused, its "Ten Reasons" had not really been answered, or even addressed. Instead, its opponents had launched a vitriolic attack on the character of those who stood in their path. The radicals applied the epithets "racist" and "bigot" not only to anyone who supported my ideas, but also to those who printed them or defended my right to express them. The ideas themselves were stigmatized as an infection the campus must mobilize to repel.

I decided to respond to these attacks by visiting the Berkeley campus, as well as other schools where the ads had appeared. It was the only way to break the quarantine. I decided to give my appearances a theatrical flourish and call them a "freedom tour." It was a way of going "in your face" to my accusers and emphasizing the issue, free speech, which had now become the heart of the debate.

I had already received an invitation from the College Republican club at Berkeley and a conservative campus paper called the *California Patriot*. Ben Carrasco, the editor of the *Patriot*, volunteered to organize the event and introduce me. Like Hernandez, Carrasco was the son of an immigrant Mexican family. His father had become the city manager of Austin, Texas, at the age of thirty-four, a fact that Carrasco made part of his résumé. "I've seen hard work and persistence pay off," he told the *Los Angeles Times;* "my dad is the embodiment of that." When asked by a reporter why he had chosen to be "an ideological minority on an overwhelmingly liberal campus," Carrasco said: "My family has always stressed patriotism, education, honesty and hard work. I like to think those are conservative values."[26]

Carrasco's attitude towards the "sensitivity" ethos of the Berkeley campus was similarly contrarian: "Kids can be mean, even when they're kidding around. I've been called the usual ethnic slurs, but I just shrug it

---

25. The student papers generally are independently owned and only partially associated with the universities themselves.
26. Dickey, "An Uncivil Discourse."

off. After all, I'm a hardened foe of political correctness so I'd be the last one to complain about stupid comments that generally mean nothing except stupidity."

When my ad appeared, Berkeley was already in the throes of a controversy over the university's admissions policy, which had already put Carrasco and the *Patriot* at odds with the left. The source of the conflict was the California Civil Rights Initiative (Proposition 209), overwhelmingly endorsed by California voters in 1996. Under the terms of the initiative, race could no longer be taken into account in granting admissions to otherwise underqualified college applicants. Coinciding with my scheduled appearance, the left was planning demonstrations to pressure university officials to defy the law and return to racial preferences. Adopting a strategy that was positively Orwellian, they were organizing students whom the university was paying to recruit minorities, urging them to do an about-face and warn these minorities not to apply to the university at all.

Two days before my scheduled appearance, the radicals organized a "Black Out" which was designed to link the two events. Activists dressed in black, their mouths covered by veils, marched into classrooms to protest that blacks on campus had been "attacked" and "ignored." A flier they handed out identified my ad and "racist" publications like the *Patriot* as reasons for their disruptions. In keeping with its normal policy of appeasing leftwing mischief, the UC administration stayed out of the picture and let the classroom obstructions proceed without reprisal.

When the masked intruders entered his classroom, public policy professor David Kirp was teaching a room full of a hundred students. Although he didn't know who the ominous figures were at first, he was accustomed to Berkeley's campus routine and could venture an educated surmise. "Rumors had recently circulated about a new round of student protests against the California Board of Regents' anti-affirmative-action policy," he explained later, "and my best guess was that the group's actions were part of that cause." For the next half-hour the masked interlopers dominated the class session as Kirp attempted to turn the incident into an object lesson. (Mathematics and physiology professors, whose classrooms were also disrupted, did not have this option.)

Previously, Kirp had agreed to let one of his students on the *Patriot* staff announce my event, as he had in other classes for students with different agendas. In his remarks, the staffer took a moment to confront the demonstrators. "It is conservatives who are really being silenced, not blacks," he said, "since at Berkeley you're labeled a racist if you dare to challenge affirmative action." In an article recounting the episode, Kirp agreed:

"Racist" is a silencing accusation, a charge like "when did you stop beating your spouse?" that brooks no effective denial. That conversation stopper is all too familiarly heard on Berkeley's balkanized campus, a factory of learning that resembles a community only when power outages are threatened or the basketball team makes it to the NCAA tournament. As Berkeley goes, so goes the rest of higher education: If you're interested in honest exchanges about controversial issues in general, and about matters of race in particular, talk radio is a better bet than any campus.[27]

Few observers missed the irony that four decades earlier, Berkeley had launched the radical era of the Sixties with a "Free Speech Movement" (FSM). The name itself was emblematic of the dopiness of PC kitsch, since there were no restrictions on speech at UC Berkeley in 1964 when the movement was launched. This did not prevent radicals from using the appealing slogan to mobilize enough bodies to occupy the university administration building, an act that resulted in the arrest of eight hundred student trespassers. It was the first "takeover" of a campus building in the history of American higher education and set the stage for similar political actions on college campuses thereafter. The repercussions of the Free Speech Movement were even greater. The radicals had challenged the very notion of the academy as an "Ivory Tower" of inquiry and reflection. Their success triggered a movement to redefine the university as an "agency of social change."

A year before my appearance, Berkeley's chancellor, Robert Berdahl, had presided over the dedication of a "Free Speech Café" to commemorate the FSM and a disruption that university officials had once condemned as a criminal act.[28] In his remarks, Berdahl showed how thoroughly university officials like him had embraced the goals of the radicals:

> The turnout for this event is wonderful. It speaks to the timelessness and power of the FSM—a power that transcends generations.... What I want to talk to you about today is the rich legacy that the FSM left for this university and other campuses across the nation and worldwide. We all know that the FSM impacted universities in a historic way.

---

27. David Kirp, "When a Classroom Protest Becomes the Lesson," *California Monthly,* June 2001. The monthly is a publication of the California Alumni Association. The article also appeared in a slightly different version in the *Chronicle of Higher Education.*

28. The café was dedicated on February 3, 2000, and situated at the university's undergraduate library. On April 13, 2001, with suitable fanfare, the Bancroft Library opened a new electronic archive devoted to the Free Speech Movement. http://www.lib.berkeley.edu/BANC/FSM/chron.html.

It was true that the impact of the Free Speech Movement had been historic, but as the trials of my ad made clear, it was not in widening the sphere of free speech. The atmosphere on the Berkeley campus was actually less hospitable to minority views now than it had been in the late 1950s, when I arrived there. This was not surprising, since the FSM was ultimately not a movement about free speech. It was about the right of the political left to agitate for its agendas within the confines of the campus itself.

"Campuses in the 1950s were not political places," as one historian and New Left veteran recalls. "College administrations discouraged students from exploring serious politics, and most students were apolitical."[29] In fact, before the FSM activists occupied Berkeley's Sproul Hall, the university had required political organizations to conduct their recruiting operations outside the Sather Gate entrance that marked the campus boundary. It was a letter by Dean Katherine A. Towle reiterating this policy to student radicals, who were chafing under the restriction, that triggered the Free Speech Movement. The dean's letter stated that it was the administration's policy to "prohibit the use of University facilities 'for the purpose of soliciting party membership or supporting or opposing particular candidates or propositions in local, state or national elections ... [and to restrict to designated areas] the distribution of handbills, circulars or pamphlets.'"[30]

This policy was designed to protect the university as a place of learning and intellectual inquiry from the kind of partisan disruptions that have since become commonplace, and that require campus security police to protect politically unpopular speakers. Before the FSM, universities like Berkeley had described themselves as institutions dedicated to the "disinterested pursuit of knowledge." The policy the FSM challenged—and overthrew—was designed to separate university activities from the rough battlegrounds of the political arena.

The broken boundary was not a legal demarcation, but a line that attempted to separate the sacred from the profane. It was a line that said discourse within the university should be more civil and respectful than was possible in the world beyond. It was this protective membrane that the FSM radicals set out to puncture. "In 1964," writes New Left historian Wini Breines, "Berkeley students became involved in an explosive

---

29. Wini Breines, "The New Left and the Student Movement," in *Long Time Gone: Sixties America Then and Now,* ed. Alexander Bloom (Oxford, 2001), pp. 25, 31.
30. Bancroft Library electronic archive.

struggle over their right to engage in politics on campus."[31] This was evident from the radicals' opening battle cry, in a leaflet declaring: "The University does not deserve a response of loyalty and allegiance from you. There is only one proper response to Berkeley from undergraduates: that you ORGANIZE AND SPLIT THIS CAMPUS WIDE OPEN."[32] It was a rhetoric that marked the American university's transformation into the politicized institution it soon became.

This was the real achievement of the FSM—the insertion of ideological politics into the heart of the university community. It was dramatized in the person of the next speaker to mount the podium at the dedication of the FSM Café and be introduced by the current chancellor as "one of the individuals who was a member of the original FSM Steering Committee" and who "like so many of her peers... went on to dedicate her life to educating others and advancing human rights." This was Bettina Aptheker, daughter of a high official of the American Communist Party in its Stalinist heyday, a longtime member of the party herself, and more recently a University of California professor.

The successful long march of Bettina Aptheker and her political comrades to seats of power in the university ensured that my return to Berkeley would not be simple. Three months earlier, former Israeli prime minister Benjamin Netanyahu had been forced to cancel an off-campus appearance because of the threat of violence from local activists.[33] The previous semester a conservative activist named Dan Flynn had been invited by the *California Patriot* to speak about convicted murderer Mumia Abu Jamal and was attacked by the same parties. Mumia had become a cause of the campus left and "Free Mumia" protests had already been held at hundreds of colleges. Mumia himself had been a commencement speaker (via tape) at four institutions. To his speech at Berkeley, Flynn brought a copy of his pamphlet, *Cop Killer: How Mumia Abu-Jamal Conned Millions into Believing He Was Framed*.[34] While campus police looked on, a mob of protesters positioned themselves at the front of the auditorium and shouted Flynn down, physically intimidated his supporters, and then stole and destroyed the pamphlets he had brought with him.

---

31. Breines, "The New Left."
32. Bancroft Library electronic archive.
33. *San Francisco Chronicle*, 29 November 2000.
34. Available from Accuracy in Academia, a think tank in Washington, D.C. Among other obvious facts, Flynn pointed out that Mumia's brother was present at the scene of the crime, but in nearly twenty years had not once said that Mumia was innocent of the brutal murder.

The fiasco was not unusual for conservative speakers. In 1994 Brandeis withdrew an invitation to former U.N. ambassador Jeanne Kirkpatrick when the faculty expressed their hostility towards her because of her opposition to Communist dictatorships and guerrilla movements in Central America during the 1980s. Threatened violence from student leftists at the University of Texas caused the cancellation of a speech by Henry Kissinger on campus in February 2000. In 1998, Flynn's organization, Accuracy in Academia, had attempted to hold a weekend conference in the Faculty Club at Columbia University. Among the speakers were Dinesh D'Souza, the author of *Illiberal Education,* a famous critique of political correctness, and Ward Connerly and Candace DeRussy, who were both university trustees. Before it got started, the conference was attacked by a chanting mob of leftist protesters. Despite the fact that Columbia had been paid for the use of its premises, campus police ignored the protesters and—under university orders—shut the conference down.[35]

Normally the left had no need to resort to such violent tactics; unless conservative speakers are celebrities, like Kirkpatrick and Kissinger, they do not attract much campus attention. Since the left generally controls student speakers' programs and funds, and since the faculty is almost universally hostile, conservatives are effectively quarantined before they arrive. Professors who regularly require students to attend appearances by speakers from the left often organize boycotts of those conservative events that manage to find funding. Campus papers do not make an effort to publicize these events (as they do for events and speakers of the left), and the advertising fliers posted by conservatives are regularly defaced (often with swastikas) and torn down.

Having spoken at dozens of college campuses over the years, I had seen these conditions firsthand. But this time my visit to Berkeley was bound to be different. The ad had made me momentarily famous on campus, and the left was determined to prevent me from making my case to an audience outside the conservative ghetto. As the Dan Flynn fiasco had made clear, moreover, I could not count on the campus police to maintain order and protect my safety.

Flynn was a burly ex-marine and had survived his ordeal without being attacked. But I had additional considerations to take into account in visiting Berkeley. The Bay Area was home to the Black Panther Party,

---

35. Dan Flynn, "Twelve Cases of Campus Censorship," www.frontpagemagazine.com. The conference moved to an off-campus facility to conduct its business. Cf. "Campus Brown Shirts," in David Horowitz, *Hating Whitey and Other Progressive Causes* (Dallas, 2000). Also *One Hundred Cases of Campus Censorship* (pamphlet), available from the Center for the Study of Popular Culture, Los Angeles.

which years ago—as I have already mentioned—murdered a friend of mine named Betty Van Patter. The tragedy eventually resulted in my departure from the left (and from Berkeley) and in my lifelong campaign to bring the truth about her murder to light. Several Panther leaders, at least one of them involved in her death, were familiar faces on the campus circuit and received a sizeable portion of their income from official speaking engagements at universities like Berkeley. The Oakland Panthers had not been a functioning group for more than twenty years, at least since the group's gangster leader, Huey Newton, was killed in 1989, in a drug burn on the mean streets of Oakland where he had grown up. But the Dr. Huey P. Newton Foundation, with a million-dollar capital investment from Stanford University (which had bought his "papers"), was a functioning base for Panther veterans. Former Panther field marshall David Hilliard, who had spent a year in jail for threatening President Nixon's life, was the head of the foundation and running for a seat on the Oakland City Council. Congresswoman Barbara Lee, whom I had worked with when she was Newton's political operative, was now the very radical Democrat representing the Berkeley-Oakland district in the United States House of Representatives.

Given this iceberg under the tip of my appearance, I decided to hire a professional security firm headed by two former Bay Area policemen, Terry Brown and Eric Fitzgerald. Both Terry and Eric were black but, unlike my student attackers, their judgments weren't formed by ideological clichés. They had lengthy experience in the real world of high-crime zones like East Palo Alto and the lockdown facilities of the maximum-security prison at Pelican Bay. Their profession had made them students of human character. They knew by what measures to assess me, and were not about to be seduced by the slanders of the left. Within weeks of our acquaintance, we were friends. I learned to respect the methodical way they went about their task, and was grateful for the seriousness with which they took their responsibilities, and the way they made me feel safe in their hands.

Hernandez's editorial appeared at the beginning of March. A week later, on March 8, I wrote a letter to the same Chancellor Berdahl who had introduced Bettina Aptheker. I observed that I was a fairly well-known writer and TV commentator, and asked him to attend my speech and to introduce me. I noted the hostile reaction the announcement of my appearance was already receiving from some segments of the university community. I then turned to the particular concerns I had about the event:

Dan Flynn of Accuracy in Academia was an invited speaker at your campus last semester... [but] was shouted down, threatened, verbally assaulted, and had his books burned by students while campus police watched.... I am a Berkeley alumnus and am appalled at the situation you have allowed to develop at my alma mater, in which speakers can be harassed and their books burned while campus authorities look on as though such behavior was normal or even acceptable at an institution of higher learning.

I then asked for the chancellor's help:

I would like your immediate assurance, that I will be civilly treated on my arrival on your campus.... I would like you or an officer of the university whom the students are bound to respect to introduce my talk, and to be present for its duration, to ensure a proper attitude of respect. I hope you will do this for every other speaker who comes to your campus with views that might be unpopular among what seems to be an organized and determined few, who would deny a hearing to those with whom they disagree.

I sent the letter to Berdahl with a copy to Ward Connerly, a regent of the university, a friend, and the man who had done more to challenge the smelly little orthodoxies of racial preferences at UC and in the United States than any other individual. I'd had no prior communication with Ward before the ad appeared, but in the furor that followed he immediately announced that he would no longer give interviews to reporters from the *Daily Californian,* as was his custom, because of their "retreat from the fundamental principle of free speech. There is nothing in the ad that offends the First Amendment so much that the *Daily Cal* has to cave in to a bunch of racial extortionists." Ward then endorsed the ad itself: "By the way, I happen to agree with Horowitz's position on reparations, which is shared by millions of Americans."[36] It was a serious blow to the paper, then focusing on admissions policy in which Connerly was a major player, and the only gesture of support anyone connected with any university was going to give me.

Berdahl did not respond directly to my appeal, but had his assistant chancellor, John Cummins, reply instead. In an e-mail that arrived three days before my scheduled appearance, Cummins insinuated that I was nothing more than a provocateur. My ad, he wrote, was not really a response to any reparations supporters at Berkeley. There was, he said,

---

36. *Daily Californian,* 9 March 2001.

"no active discussion of such claims on this campus" prior to my advertisement.

> You indicate that, in response to the "swift and hostile" reaction to the advertisement, "other voices from the community have spoken up, demonstrating the desire for a genuine dialogue on this subject." No demand for "dialogue" existed prior to your effort to provoke it.[37]

In fact, as I eventually learned from my student hosts, before my ad appeared several professors had already lectured their captive classroom audiences on the need for reparations. There was even a "Reparations Awareness Day" that had recently been organized by the left during Black History Month. Had the chancellor remonstrated with the organizers of that event? Did he ever concern himself with the disruptions of university routines in behalf of Palestinian radicalism, or efforts to gain reprieves for a murderer like Mumia Abu Jamal, or any other intrusions into the academic setting? My ad was not a disruption, or an obstruction of anyone's routine. What an idea, in any event, to come from the administrative head of a renowned institution of higher learning. It was as though the chancellor's office thought I should feel guilty for attempting to make its students think about this issue.

In fact, this was Chancellor Berdahl's own view of the situation, which was even more hostile than the attitude struck in Cummins' letter, as a profile in the *Los Angeles Times* made clear:

> Berkeley Chancellor Robert M. Berdahl speaks of Horowitz as though the man had kicked his dog. "He opened up an issue—reparations for slavery—that nobody was talking about," he says in an interview. "I said, 'Why is he doing this?' Also, [the ad] was couched in offensive language. This is a guy who acts outrageously, wants to outrage people, and then cries foul when they are outraged and offended. I think it's all perfectly ridiculous because nobody takes him seriously, except maybe himself."[38]

Berdahl's reaction confirmed the quip of my longtime writing partner Peter Collier, who had once described the modern university administrator as a cross between Saul Alinksy[39] and Neville Chamberlain. To appease the radicals, Berdahl turned a blind eye to their war against the marketplace of ideas. On the other hand, he was not going to chance a

---

37. John Cummins, letter to the author, 12 March 2001.
38. Dickey, "An Uncivil Discourse."
39. "Community organizer" and author of a book called *Rules for Radicals*.

disturbance during my visit that might tarnish his public image. His office assigned thirty campus police officers to monitor the event. But, even then, as Cummins made clear, there would be no guarantees:

> March 15 is the day upon which the supporters of Affirmative Action will be protesting at the meeting of the Regents of the University of California. It is a moment when passions will be very high on issues of race. Your appearance will add fuel to a controversy that is already hot. That is your right. I cannot guarantee that you will not be shouted at, because the right of free expression also belongs to those who disagree with you. I cannot guarantee that you will not be treated rudely because there is no law against rude behavior.

It was not a matter of law, of course. It was a matter of decorum, and universities like Berkeley did have rules—and plenty of them—requiring appropriate behavior to satisfy the concerns of the left. Perhaps the most famous incident of this political correctness was the attempt to punish a freshman at the University of Pennsylvania for referring to a gaggle of raucous undergraduates who were disturbing his studies as "water buffalo." Only an outcry from the non-campus media, a bevy of ACLU lawyers and a couple of courageous faculty defenders managed to save him from a star chamber proceeding and possible expulsion.[40] Some of the campus rules, including those respecting hostile gender attentions and looks (referred to as "lookism"), and speech codes that barred "insensitive" remarks were so extreme that they were successfully challenged in courts of law.[41]

I had no intention of inflaming students who were planning demonstrations to support racial preferences. In fact, the UC Regents were meeting in Los Angeles, which would draw potential protesters hundreds of miles away from my event. But it was interesting how quick and consistent university officials were to blame the bad behavior of the campus left on the very targets of their intolerance.

■　■

My speech had been scheduled as an evening event. When I arrived in the dark at a rear entrance to the Life Sciences Building, the chief of the campus police informed my security that a demonstration was in progress at the front of the building. The organizing group, I later learned, was the Spartacist Youth League, which would be orchestrating similar pickets at

---

40. Alan Kors and Harvey Silverglate, The Shadow University: The Betrayal of Liberty on America's Campuses (New York, 1998), ch. 1, "The Water Buffalo Affair."
41. Martin P. Golding, *Free Speech on Campus.*

other schools.[42] I remembered the Spartacists from my radical days as a Trotskyist splinter group, which had supported the Soviet invasion of Hungary in 1956. As blunt as they were otiose, the Spartacists described themselves on their website as an "International Communist League" and their organization as "a proletarian, revolutionary and internationalist tendency committed to the task of building Leninist parties as national sections of a democratic-centralist international. Our aim is the achievement of new October Revolutions—nothing else, nothing other, nothing less."[43]

Parading with their placards in front of the Life Sciences Building and pretending to be the voice of oppressed African-Americans, the Spartacists provided the images that were later featured on TV news segments and in national magazines like *Newsweek*. Their chants were as colorful as they were antique:

David Horowitz, the Ku Klux Klan—It's all part of the bosses' plan.

Black liberation through socialist revolution!

I was whisked in through a back entrance to a "holding room" where I was to stay until my speech. All hallways were secured by uniformed officers so that no stray students might stumble across my path. When I had to leave the holding room briefly to go to the bathroom, I was accompanied by six armed guards who checked the stalls before I was allowed to enter. The experience was surreal. The bracing Berkeley campus of my youth had been replaced in the forty years since I studied there by an atmosphere lacking only bomb-sniffing dogs to complete the sense of menace it conveyed to "the Other." The only comparison that came to mind was that of a neighborhood once habitable and inviting for evening strollers, which had become occupied by roving thugs.

Before speaking, I was interviewed by the local channel, KTVU, as well as CNN, FoxNews, ABC and the local and campus press. I said it was tragic that a few "campus fascists" should make it impossible to discuss ideas freely on a college campus. When I entered the large lecture hall, the front rows of the audience of about five hundred cheered. They were answered by catcalls and hoots from the radicals ganged up in the back.

---

42. These included the universities of California (Davis), Chicago and Massachusetts, Boston University and the Massachusetts Institute of Technology.

43. "The ICL bases itself on Marxist historical, dialectical materialism and seeks in particular to carry forward the international working-class perspectives of Marxism developed in the theory and practice of the Bolshevik leaders V. I. Lenin and L. D. Trotsky and embodied in the decisions of the first four Congresses of the Communist International as well as key documents of the Fourth International such as the 'Transitional Program' (1938) and 'War and the Fourth International' (1934)."

I guessed that about half of my supporters were students while others had responded to a call put out by a local radio talk show. The opposition included many overage radicals from the Spartacist Youth League, the Young Socialists and other groups. About forty students and several of the professional organizers were black.

After Ben Carrasco introduced me, he put a mike into my hand. I paced across the raised lectern, driven by nervous energy, and began speaking to the now quieted crowd. "This situation reminds me of an old Richard Pryor album," I began. "On the cover, Pryor is cowering before a crowd of hooded Klansmen who are about to lynch him. The cover line is: 'Is it something I said?' Actually... it *was* something I said."[44]

"It was a national disgrace," I continued, "that ideas reasonably expressed in a college newspaper should produce the kind of reaction that would convince a university administration to provide armed guards to protect a speaker from bodily harm. The atmosphere on campuses like Berkeley is less free than it was when I was an undergraduate Marxist at Columbia in the McCarthy Fifties. This is because the witch-hunters then were politicians who were outside the university community, which was itself hostile to McCarthyism and opposed to intolerance. These attitudes protected unpopular figures like me. But now the witch-hunters and the commissars of political correctness are inside the university, sitting on its faculties and wielding the power of its bureaucracies. Now there is no such protection for a dissenting opinion, like mine."

I confessed my own responsibility in contributing to this development. "Forty years ago I was a graduate student at Berkeley and one of the campus radicals who were agitating to make the university a hospitable arena for political ideologues like those who are protesting my speech tonight. Thus, my appearance tonight can be seen, in part, as an attempt to undo what I, and others like me, are responsible for. I am here to make a stand *against* the atmosphere of intolerance I helped to create.

"Today this intolerance takes the form of a 'racial McCarthyism.' Just as the accusation of Communism was career-threatening in the 1950s, so is the imputation of racism now. Then it was Communists under the beds; now it's a racist in every head. Of course, there *were* in fact Communists

---

44. The speech that follows is not a verbatim account, but a composite of the speeches I gave in the twelve appearances I made in the weeks ahead. The main body of my presentation was the same for every school, but the emphases, anecdotes and arguments were tailored for the specific audiences. After my tour was over, I checked my memory of the Richard Pryor album cover from an image on Amazon.com. It turned out I was mistaken. Pryor is robed and surrounded by monk-like figures and is about to be burned at the stake as a heretic. In some ways a better image even, but in another sense obviously not.

then, who were indeed part of an international conspiracy that was orchestrated from Moscow. I know, because I was raised in a Communist household. The recent opening of the Soviet archives has established these facts now for all to see. But McCarthy also used the accusation of Communism to wound and destroy political enemies who were not Communists, which is why his name has fallen into such bad repute. Campus radicals are now employing McCarthy's techniques to oppose my ad. There is not a racist statement that they can point to in the ad, but that does not deter them from calling it 'racist.' The idea is to demonize me and to intimidate others from even considering my point of view.

"The fear of being falsely identified as a racist is a pervasive fact of campus life. Not a single scholar of slavery has come forward to support the obviously true historical statements my ad contained. My opponents are making ludicrous arguments, such as the claim that black slavery in Africa was not really bad, that the Civil War was not really about slavery, and that the world movement against slavery was not an invention of Europeans and Christians. The reason for the professors' silence is obvious. They are afraid of becoming involved because they know this will make them the targets of false accusations of *racism* too. It is the same fear that caused the *Daily Californian* editors to capitulate to the left's intolerant demands.

"In the nation beyond the university, everyone who isn't black or isn't politically left is walking on eggshells now around the issue of race. We have just had hearings in the Senate over the nomination of John Ashcroft to be attorney general. During these hearings, the nation has been treated to the spectacle of Ashcroft's interrogation by senators like Ted Kennedy to this effect: *Mr. Ashcroft, are you now or have you ever been pro-slavery?* An appropriate response would have been ridicule and laughter. But no one laughed. Even Ashcroft attempted to defend himself by saying 'If I had been in the Civil War, I would have fought with Grant.' It's 2001 everybody! Yet in 2001, fear of being tarred by the racial brush made everyone deferential to a preposterous suspicion.[45]

"On university campuses, as you know, the situation is much worse. Speech codes, disciplinary measures and kangaroo courts have been created

---

45. The actual questions to Ashcroft may have been more subtly put, but their implication was not. The pretext for the questions was that Ashcroft had given an interview to the *Southern Partisan Review* in which he had expressed, in passing, admiration for the loyalty to their cause displayed by Confederate statesmen and generals. This was a commonplace observation about a figure like Robert E. Lee—cf. Jay Winik's *April 1865: The Month That Saved America* (New York, 2001)—but it almost cost him confirmation as attorney general of the United States.

to purge unclean thoughts and expressions from students and professors alike.[46] The failure of the adults at this university to defend the reasonableness of my views (not just my right to express them), and to condemn the vicious slanders against me is a clear warning that reasonably expressed opinions that the left doesn't like will get a similar response.

"Unlike the students in this audience, I cannot be punished by the university for my views. But anyone involved in the life of this campus knows that expressing similar views can jeopardize their careers. The prudent will take note and keep their counsel. How can you run a university like this? How can there be freedom of inquiry into controversial issues, if there is a witch-hunt in progress? In coming to Berkeley I am fighting a battle for *your* freedom, *your* right to an education, as much as I am fighting for my own."

I then confronted the issue of minority feelings that had been so prominent in the attacks on my ad.

"The most common charge against my ad is that it is offensive and hurts people's feelings. Some black students say they have been made to feel 'unwelcome' because of the ideas expressed. If this was anywhere but a modern college campus these complaints would be preposterous. They're hurt because of *ideas?*

"Why would any self-respecting person want to say that they can't handle ideas they disagree with? Why would a university encourage college students to say such a thing? What kind of an educational lesson is that? It's patronizing. It's infantilizing. Professors and administrators who claim to care about black students should be telling those who complain to them: 'Stand up. You can take it. And you can give it back!' I am confident that no self-respecting black person who has not been brainwashed by the academic left would say: *Oh gosh. The ideas in that ad are hurting my feelings. Who will protect me?* Yet that is exactly the demeaning response that administrators, professors and editors like Daniel Hernandez are encouraging in African-American students on this campus.

"It's all part of the left's credo that speech is power. In this university, of course, it's obviously effective. By running to the *Daily Californian* and whining, leftists persuaded the editors to accuse me of bigotry, and thereby relieved themselves of the need to come up with a single idea in response to my ten points. It's a seductive proposition. If so minded, you can attend a great university but skip the entire curriculum of logic,

---

46. Cf. Harvey Silverglate and Alan Kors, *The Shadow University,* for a detailed study of this apparatus and its consequences, and books like Daphne Patai's *Heterophobia: Sexual Harassment and the Future of Feminism* (New York, 1998).

evidence, and rational discourse—and simply call people with ideas you don't like 'racists' instead.

"The whole 'sensitivity' idea is based on a collective fantasy that only academics could believe. It assumes that minority students have entered an environment in which they are embattled and oppressed. The opposite is more likely true. Entrance requirements have been rigged in their favor. They are given scholarships and stipends, based on their victim status, even if their economic circumstances (not to mention grade scores) don't justify it. Skin color is what determines everything. Designated minorities are singled out in the orientation process as members of a group the university is pledged to protect. Its humanity depends on it. They know that if they experience anything that seems like racial or ethnic harassment, or any situation that makes them feel 'uncomfortable,' they can come to authorities confident that an impressive apparatus of disciplinary sanctions will be at their service and provide them justice. When their course work is completed, they even have separate graduations to mark them as special and apart. At this university and others, the national creed of *e pluribus unum* has been reversed. It has become 'out of one, many.' And among the many, minorities are a privileged caste."[47]

Then I asked my student audience the question directly: "Would you rather be a minority student at this university whom someone called a name, or a white student accused of calling someone a name? It's obviously a no-brainer. If you are black and you accuse someone of calling you a name, that other person is already in trouble. The realities of power at universities like Berkeley are exactly the opposite of what its guardians claim. The epithets flung at my ad are the most destructive weapons of discourse available. Their purpose is to crush an idea the left can't handle."

As I was approaching the end of this thought, my eye caught the figure of Assistant Chancellor John Cummins sitting in a back row among the disgruntled left. I had been advised that Cummins would be in the audience, but it wasn't until this moment that I was able to pick him out. In a gambit that later caused friction with one of my student hosts, I looked directly at him and said:

"The assistant chancellor of this university is sitting there in the back row as part of the problem. You, sir, should be up on this stage instructing your students in the behavior appropriate to a university setting. It's

---

47. My antagonist at the *Daily Californian*, Daniel Hernandez, was a case in point. He had indeed risen from real hardship to come to Berkeley, but the chancellor had personally phoned him to inform him of his acceptance. This was a powerful message that he could not help but notice and that probably fed the arrogance he later displayed. Fred Dickey, "An Uncivil Discourse."

fine that everybody seems to be well behaved at this point, but that's because my student hosts insisted on a 'no tolerance' policy that has so far made this possible. This policy has to be made normal. [Attendees were told on entering that they would be removed if they caused any disruption.] The presence of the police is the result of a long-running dereliction of duty by the administration of this university. It's your responsibility to create an appropriate learning environment. You need to adopt a zero tolerance policy for the obstruction of speakers. You need to stop patronizing minorities, and hold all students to standards of civility and respect."

Cummins just sat there, small and inconsequential in his seat in the back row, the perfect embodiment of the university's abdication.

I now turned to the reparations issue itself. "Slavery was a crime against humanity, and is a blot on the American record. I fully support reparations for former slaves and their children. Unfortunately they are no longer with us. Even though no payment can make up for the injury of slavery, American slaves should have been compensated when they were freed. Instead, they were even denied the forty acres and a mule they had been promised. This was a betrayal, as were the years of segregation and discrimination that followed.

"But the injury of slavery is far in the past. The reparations claim has to be assessed as a political proposal, in terms of its practical impact now. This complicates the issue. How can you explain to José Martinez, who may have come to this country in the last ten years, and who is struggling to put bread on the table for his family, that he has to pay reparations for an institution that has been dead for more than a hundred years, and which neither he nor his ancestors were ever a part of? How will you tell him that he has to pay those reparations to people like Johnny Cochran and Jesse Jackson who are multimillionaires, or to others who are doing better than he is, simply because they are black? Anyone should be able to see that the reparations claim is really a prescription for racial division and ethnic strife.

"Reparations for slavery will not benefit African-Americans, but will isolate them, and set others against them. Demanding reparations is like saying to other Americans: *You* are responsible for slavery and segregation and discrimination, whether you believe it or not. *Your* racism is responsible for the fact that some of us are poor, and some of us are criminals, and some of us lack educational credentials. *Your* racism did this to us. Now, *give us money!*

"Reparations is a politically stupid idea. Americans have already shown that they can be generous in supporting efforts to make up the deficits inflicted by injustices of the past. Acknowledgement should be made of that fact. Americans have been willing to invest large sums of money to help blacks and others who have fallen behind. But they are not going to respond generously to an indictment of their own humanity and good intentions.

"How can America's diverse communities be brought together on the basis of the claim that one group, the majority of whom are doing well in terms of the American average, is owed by all the others? How can African-Americans feel at home in this country, if they are constantly being told how badly this country is treating them, and that every setback they experience is the responsibility of everyone else? How can black Americans (or any group) be 'empowered' by constantly being told they are victims, and that their destiny is controlled by someone else?

"The answer is they can't. In the name of 'social justice,' so-called progressives are sending a crippling message to black students at this university. A sense of achievement and a sense of one's ability to prevail in adverse circumstances are essential elements of the self-confidence and self-esteem that make all success possible.

"One can actually look at the history of black people in America and come up with the precise opposite of the gloom and doom picture that reparations partisans prefer. It's all a matter of perspective. One can always take the view that the American glass is half empty. How about looking at the same glass from a different angle?

"One hundred thirty-six years ago, most black people in America had nothing. Their ancestors were dragged here in chains. They had been stripped of their language, their culture, and their connection to a communal history. When slavery came to an end, they had to start from scratch. Yet in a mere two or three generations—*despite* segregation, *despite* discrimination—they have created a large middle class, changed the shape of American culture, risen to great political heights and collectively constitute one of the richest 'economies' on earth. This is an astonishing achievement. But if you mention it on a university campus, you will be called 'insensitive' and 'anti-black.'"

When I finished, I thanked the audience for their respectful attention and opened the floor for questions. Until then, the crowd had been fairly well behaved. But the organizers of the event made a mistake. They had arranged for hand-held mikes to be brought up the aisles to facilitate questions. Lines had formed in the back half of the audience where the left was seated. An older black man, who identified himself as a Muslim immigrant, immediately departed from the stated format, which was to ask questions and not make speeches. He accused me directly of being a "racist" because I "discounted the suffering of blacks." This was just the opening for a litany of racial grief. But after he had spoken for a while, though he never asked a question, I was able to talk over him and get him to sit down.

Two more people got up to accuse me of racism. Then a man who looked to be in his forties, whom I later discovered was a lawyer and the head of an organization called the National Council of African Men, started a serious verbal confrontation. When he had gone on for a while I asked him to formulate a question or conclude his speech. But his oratory went on, and it seemed to me he was just warming up. I tried again to get him to wrap it up, but it was a test of wills that I was clearly losing. Others in the back had begun to shout catcalls at the stage, and I wondered what might happen if the man continued much longer. I tried again, more urgently, saying others were waiting to ask questions as well, but to no avail.

Meanwhile, the police in attendance were growing nervous at the breakdown of order, and they asked Ben Carrasco to shut off his mike. Carrasco's attempt to do so produced howls of "censorship" and jeers from the back, and he quickly retreated. The surge of emotional energy was alarming, and indicated how quickly the situation could get out of control. I tried to think of ways to regain the platform, which was now my antagonist's. I was increasingly apprehensive about what might happen next. I looked around for the police, but saw none. I didn't want to give up and leave, which I knew would be used against me, but neither did I want to risk an outburst in which the howls could turn into a scuffle and the scuffle into mayhem in which people might get hurt. I came to a decision, and made a last appeal. "If you won't let anyone else speak," I shouted over the speechmaker who was still in full throat, "this meeting will be over!" It brought no response. Nodding to my security, I said "We're out of here," and left.

In interviews with the media, the protesters pounced on this exit as a flight from the battle. But it was hardly that. Unlike the people sitting in the audience, I had personal security guards who would ensure my safety. An eruption of violence would have gained the event enormous publicity and a much greater platform for the views I wished to promote. But I did not want to accomplish this by risking the safety of others. Looking back, if I had to make the decision again, I would do the same.

Censorship and cowardice are not the values the University of Wisconsin should be promoting. A university is supposed to confirm us as adults by helping us to pursue knowledge. Instead, UW administrators wish to act as speech inquisitors, protecting us as children from the menace of other ideas.
    Hasdai Westbrook, *The Badger Herald*,
    May 10, 2001

THREE

THE STUDENTS (WISCONSIN)

F our days after Daniel Hernandez's apology appeared in the Berkeley student newspaper, a mob of chanting students attacked the offices of the *Badger Herald* at the University of Wisconsin to protest the same ad placed there.[48] The demonstrators were organized by a "Multicultural Student Coalition," whose leader, a senior named Tshaka Barrows, was the son of the university's vice chancellor for student affairs. "One hundred screaming protesters outside the doors of a small newspaper office can be intimidating," *Herald* editor Julie Bosman wrote in the *Wall Street Journal* afterwards. "The protesters swarmed outside the office of my paper [after] marching across campus, brandishing placards that read '*Badger Herald* Racist.' They demonstrated for more than an hour, demanding my resignation as editor."[49]

The angry crowd waited outside the offices for a representative of the paper to come out. When none showed, members of the crowd turned on the *Badger Herald* reporter covering the protest:

---

48. The ad actually appeared on the same day, February 28, that it appeared in the *Daily Californian*. The demonstration took place on March 6, after *Herald* editors rejected by a vote of 5–0 the coalition's demands.
49. Julie Bosman, "The (No) Free Speech Movement," *Wall Street Journal,* 14 March 2001.

A black woman asked the white reporter how she would feel if their positions were reversed. The reporter, who did not give her name, turned her back to her heckler, who continued to egg her on through a megaphone: "You're a reporter! Get used to it! Get fucking used to it!" As the young woman walked away in tears, one protester walked up to her. "I'm sorry, I don't agree with that," she told the reporter.[50]

The protestors also demanded that the chancellor's office bar the *Badger Herald* from campus newsstands,[51] and that it publish a statement authored by the Multicultural Student Coalition, denouncing the paper as a "perpetrator of racist propaganda."[52] Tshaka Barrows told one reporter: "As long as the *Herald* is allowed to rain racism down on us we must fight, we must resist with everything we have."[53] Another protester, junior Becky Wasserman, told the same reporter: "Freedom of speech does not mean you can infringe on other people's freedom, right? We're dealing with hate speech, and that doesn't fall under freedom."

On March 14, a rival campus paper indulgent of multicultural sensibilities, the *Daily Cardinal*, printed the coalition's statement attacking the *Herald* as "racist." In a newspaper interview, *Cardinal* business manager Eric Storck defended its publication. "We made the decision because we felt that as a newspaper it's our position to provide our pages for anybody to purchase."[54] This privilege did not extend to me, however. My office had sent the *Cardinal* a copy of the ad, which Storck rejected on March 21, explaining, "After extensive deliberation, we concluded this advertisement is offensive to our readership and running it would be inappropriate." The letter also claimed that "The *Daily Cardinal* has no problem representing all viewpoints related to this issue in our editorial content" and invited me to submit "content" to the opinion editor concerning "[my] position on slavery reparations."[55] I did this, but the op-ed I wrote was also rejected.

The headline for the Multicultural Student Coalition statement read "*Badger Herald:* UW Madison *Independent* Racist Propaganda Machine." Noting that "black students have stormed the office of the *Badger Herald*

---

50. Aaron Nathans, "100 Protest *Badger Herald* Ad, Cartoon; 2 Items Called Racist; Group's Ad Rejected," *Capital Times*, 7 March 2001.

51. Like the *Daily Californian*, the *Badger Herald* is an independent, student-run newspaper.

52. The statement was endorsed by the coalition and eleven other leftist organizations.

53. Nathans, "100 Protest *Badger Herald* Ad."

54. Sharif Durhams, "UW Students Protest Reparations Ad," *Milwaukee Journal-Sentinel*, 6 March 2001.

55. Letter from Eric Storck to Bruce Donaldson, 21 March 2001.

on several occasions over the past couple of years," the statement turned to the editors' current offenses. This included a "racially offensive" cartoon the *Herald* had also published, featuring a swastika and members of the Ku Klux Klan:

> The Ku Klux Klan comic and the Anti-Reparations for Slavery advertisement are prime examples of the newspaper's long standing tradition of attacking the character of people of color, and their history in this country. The KKK represents a racist ideology that historically operated to violate the civil rights and liberties of non-whites through violent action. The KKK cartoon that appeared in the *Badger Herald* reflects this same racist agenda. Context alone cannot filter out or justify the traumatic effects of a KKK cartoon with images of a swastika that offends Whites, Asians, Latinos, Blacks, Native Americans, and Jews.[56]

The cartoon, by *Herald* staff artist Adam Rust, was actually an attack on conformity and a send-up of the Klan. It portrayed a cluster of hooded KKK members gathered around a podium with a swastika painted on it. One Klan member's robe and hood was decorated with flowers and rabbits. Another Klan member was saying to him: "You should really get yourself some solid white sheets."

The coalition statement showed no greater sense of discernment when it came to dismissing my ad:

> The racist advertisement that recently ran in the *Herald* is a bold slap in the face to students of color who have to deal with the daily effects of the mis-education that the advertisement produced. These attacks are masked as examples of free speech that have historically been used to reinforce white dominance, which is one form of white supremacy. This type of speech has a debilitating impact on the lives of those students of color who are being targeted by race. Intent is never an adequate justification for impact.

Like Berkeley, Madison had been an epicenter of 1960s radicalism, whose veterans had gone from its "revolutionary" battles to tenured positions in the university hierarchies. The *Badger Herald* was itself an institution launched by other Sixties activists who belonged to members of Young Americans for Freedom, an organization of the Goldwater right. Over the years it had evolved into a more centrist journal, while retaining a conservative edge.

---

56. *Daily Cardinal*, 14 March 2001.

The *Herald* editors explained their position on the controversy in an editorial that ran on March 6:

> At the *Badger Herald,* we only regret that the editors of the *Daily Californian* allowed themselves to give in to pressure in a manner that unfortunately violated their professional integrity and journalistic duty to protect speech with which they disagree.
>
> The knee-jerk response by the *Californian* is frighteningly indicative of the growing tendency of college newspapers to allow the opinions they publish to be stomped out for fear of being called names. . . .
>
> We will not apologize for the publication of the advertisement, last month's controversial cartoon that belittled Ku Klux Klan members or any other controversial subject matter that would require us to compromise someone's First Amendment rights.

Defending itself against the attacks of racism, the *Herald* editors singled out the coalition's leader, Tshaka Barrows:

> Leading the current charge against the *Herald* is Multicultural Student Coalition chair Tshaka Barrows. Last December, the *Herald* recognized Barrows for his work as an advocate of diversity. The *Herald* also broke a story last spring exposing a former ASM member for a racist e-mail he wrote to Barrows. While Barrows certainly has a responsibility to the students he represents, he should also remember the *Herald*'s longstanding and ongoing efforts to stand up for the interests of students of color through open and uncensored discourse.

This editorial, of course, was not met by understanding. While the apologetic stance of Daniel Hernandez at Berkeley limited the attacks against the *Daily Cal* to the issue containing the ad, at the *Herald* the attacks continued throughout the semester. "Several students have witnessed others throwing away stacks of *Heralds* from their racks in university buildings," Bosman wrote in her *Wall Street Journal* column, "while several *Herald* staff members have retrieved heaps of bundled papers from garbage cans in the same buildings. How ironic it is that the diversity of viewpoints the activists are demanding is trashed along with the open forum in which it can be represented."[57]

Letters to the *Herald* editors ran overwhelmingly in favor of their decision. The nation's press, which had sharply criticized Daniel Hernandez for capitulating to the protesters' demands, gave the *Herald* editors strong support. "Anyone who doubts that the Constitution is a living

---

57. Bosman, "The (No) Free Speech Movement."

document need look no further than the offices of the *Badger Herald* student newspaper at the University of Wisconsin, Madison," the *Milwaukee Journal-Sentinel* editorialized. *Herald* editors Julie Bosman and Alexander Conant were invited to write op-ed pieces in the *Wall Street Journal* and the *New York Times* and to make appearances on MSNBC and C-Span. They saw their "courage" and "principles" applauded in *USA Today,* the *Wall Street Journal,* the *Milwaukee Journal-Sentinel* and the *Wisconsin State Journal,*[58] which also criticized the university administration and the vice chancellor for student affairs, Paul Barrows, for their own positions. Said the *State Journal,*

> Sadly, the vice chancellor for student affairs on the UW-Madison campus has said that if he was editor of the *Badger Herald,* he would not have authorized the Horowitz ad. Is there any better evidence of the importance of an independent press?
>
> When it comes to the First Amendment on the UW-Madison campus, leadership on protecting it will come first from students such as those at the *Badger Herald.* It will not come from administrators who value the protection of feelings above all.[59]

The young staffers at the *Herald* were encouraged by the favorable coverage they received. "The praise is as overwhelming as it is unexpected," managing editor Alexander Conant wrote. "While it seems naïve to think [so] now... nobody expected the national acclaim. At most, we fretted our non-apology could antagonize the protesters." Instead, what followed was a "predominantly positive reaction in the national media." The same was true of the public. "While the editor of the *Daily Cal* privately complained to me that he was being inundated with hate mail... we were inundated with support."[60]

The rival *Daily Cardinal* was also impacted. On March 23, it ran an editorial defending its decision to reject the ad because it "would insult students of color." The editorial continued, "The *Badger Herald* has been praised for printing the ad and upholding the First Amendment," but argued somewhat fuzzily that the issue really was "less a constitutional crusade than a quest for truth." By publishing views like mine, the *Herald* had inadvertently provided a service by which "the wider community

---

58. Alexander Conant, "The Reporters Have Become the Reported," *Badger Herald,* 27 March 2001.
59. Editorial, "*Badger Herald* Does a Free Press Proud," *Wisconsin State Journal,* 14 March 2001.
60. Conant, "The Reporters Have Become the Reported."

learns that such logically flawed and dangerous rhetoric continues to exist." Since the ad had already been published, however, the *Cardinal* editors saw no reason to publish a statement that "was most certainly offensive in its inaccuracies, fallacies and racist connotations." They declined to provide a rebuttal to even one of the ten reasons I had given for opposing reparations, or a single example of a fallacy, inaccuracy or racist connotation in anything I had written.

I tested even these intentions by submitting a second version of the ad, including material that had not previously appeared in the *Herald*. The answer was no surprise: "Once again, we regret to inform you that the *Daily Cardinal* has chosen to decline to run the advertisement your organization submitted on Wednesday, March 28, 2001. For the same reasons stated in our letter regarding your original advertisement, we conclude that this ad would be offensive to our readers." There were, of course, no "reasons" given in the previous letter.

Nonetheless, the *Cardinal* editors made a determined effort to cover both sides of the story (and cover their bases). They ran parallel interviews with Tshaka Barrows and me, and gave me the opportunity to confront them with their own hypocrisy:

> *David Horowitz:* I've read the *Cardinal* editorial. I see that it attacks me as a person whose ideas are dangerous and ignorant, yet it refuses to inform its own readers of the nature of the ideas it's attacking. This may be intellectual cowardice; it may be oversight; but it's certainly not ethical.[61]

In addition to being the leader of the Multicultural Student Coalition, Tshaka Barrows was a senior in political science and I was interested to see how he presented his case in a setting that required a little more thought than placard slogans. I quote his interview at length not only because of its relevance to the conflict at hand, but because it shows the vulgarities that shape the outlooks of the leaders of today's "multicultural" student organizations:

> *Daily Cardinal:* What is the Multicultural Student Coalition's stance on slavery reparations, and in particular, your response to Horowitz's ten points against slavery reparations?
> *Tshaka Barrows:* Reparations for slavery are just a basic first step of acknowledgement and retribution. It's taking care of a debt that's owed to African-Americans. It's an institutional acknowledgement

---

61. *Daily Cardinal*, 28 March 2001.

from a society, from a dominant group in society that it has done
wrongdoing to a people, and it intends to make an effort to deal with
the wrongdoing.

As far as the issues of slavery reparations, African-Americans, or
African people were enslaved. People want to bring up the issue that
there were slaves in Africa and that African people enslaved each other.
That's a totally different type of slavery. The American slavery and
European slavery was a slavery of dominance and violence and destruc-
tion with genocidal impacts on African peoples.[62]

The idea that African slavery, which pre-existed the Atlantic slave
trade by a thousand years, was a relatively benign institution was a standard (and wholly fallacious) debating point for reparations claimants. The
idea that only white-enforced slavery was bad paralleled the equally common claim that only white people could be racists, an argument which
Barrows also reprised:

> *Daily Cardinal:* Talk more specifically about why students-of-color
> were offended by the Horowitz ad, and what an ad of that nature
> does to the campus climate.
> *Tshaka Barrows:* When you go and open your paper, and you see a
> full-page advertisement on the last day of Black History Month, which
> not only calls into question the entire history of slavery and the impact
> it has had on African-Americans, Native Americans and other peo-
> ple of color, it's basically reducing [slavery] to an issue [of opinion].
> That's the first offense.... The other thing is people are going to take
> tests or examinations, and they see a title that specifically identifies
> anybody who is in favor of reparations as a racist, that is another
> story in itself.[63] Because one, that is a dangerous and a violent state-
> ment. There's a dominant factor in society, the media, which is con-
> trolled predominantly by white folks, telling other people of color and
> white folks who might be in favor of reparations, that to do so is
> racist. Which is not even a true statement. In order to be racist, you
> have to have the power to institutionalize your prejudice.
> *Daily Cardinal:* So is this your definition of racism?
> *Tshaka Barrows:* Racism is having the power to institutionalize your
> prejudice.[64]

---

62. *Daily Cardinal,* 28 March 2001. The interview was conducted by Jessica Peterson.
63. The title of my ad called the reparations idea "racist."
64. Not surprisingly, many black students are themselves confused. Troy Duster, a noted
    black sociologist at the University of California, Berkeley, has reported, for example,
    "When I ask black students what they mean when they claim this university is a
    racist place, they often don't know what to say." Dana Takagi, *The Retreat from
    Race: Asian American Admissions and Racial Politics* (New Brunswick: Rutgers
    University Press, 1992), p. 146.

Daily Cardinal: Does the Horowitz ad fit your definition of racism?
Tshaka Barrows: Exactly. That's why it fits. He's clearly prejudiced against African-Americans and against any of the effects of race relations in this country. And, because of the reality of our society, his prejudice was allowed to be institutionalized, and [16,000][65] of his statements were presented to our campus. He was actively, as well as the *Herald,* exercising their racism, their power to institutionalize their racism.

The second part of racism is making sure your institutionalized prejudice never comes into question. And that's why [the *Herald*] didn't print our advertisement. They had two major aspects of racism working overtime....

Daily Cardinal: Some people have criticized the Multicultural Student Coalition's ad that ran in the *Daily Cardinal* as being racist and offensive in its own right.

Tshaka Barrows: That's the dominance of society rejecting a voice that does not reflect the same dominant ideology.... Everything we put [in the ad] was based upon reality. It was based upon the historical context that we are not responsible for creating. And the fact that everyone wants to call us racist. [They are] not acknowledging the essence of what racism is. We do not have the power to institutionalize our prejudice. What we are doing is simply standing up and defending our identity....

Daily Cardinal: Horowitz said one of his complaints with your ad, and the attacks against his ad in general, is that no one has come up with a list of ten arguments countering his original ten points against slavery reparations.

Tshaka Barrows: Because that's what he wants us to do. By debating his ten points, it gives credit to what he's doing. And we know that those are credit-less points. They're unfounded. They're just inflammatory statements that are trying to draw out a fight....

Barrows also had a view of the free speech dimension of the debate:

Daily Cardinal: Do you think political correctness has stunted free speech and political debate of those with "unaccepted" or "unpopular" beliefs?

Tshaka Barrows: Free speech has been used against African-Americans for a long time. Free speech has meant freedom for white folks to say pretty much whatever they want about African-Americans and other people of color. Because of the way our society is set up, everybody

---

65. This is the circulation of the *Herald.*

does not have that same freedom of speech. So, the essence of something existing is that it exists for all in our society. Free speech does not exist for everybody.

These remarks provided a disturbing indication of what students like Barrows—a major in political science—are being taught (and not taught) in institutions of higher learning today. Equally revealing of college administrators' complicity in their aggressive naïveté was the intervention by Tshaka's father, Vice Chancellor Paul Barrows, when his son's campaign failed to force the student editors to retreat.

On May 7, as the school term was ending, a new ad appeared in the *Badger Herald*. It was signed by seventy-two members of the university administration, including the director of admissions, the dean of students and eighteen other deans, and members of the Student Life Directors who oversee the student community. The ad was placed by Ruby Paredes, executive assistant to the vice chancellor for student affairs.[66] It bore the headline "Improve Campus Climate," and began:

> We, the undersigned staff and faculty of the University of Wisconsin-Madison have been concerned about the recent incidents on campus, that are destructive to the university's efforts to create a welcoming and respectful climate for all students.

The statement referred to the cartoon about KKK conformity that had appeared in the *Herald* and had offended the coalition members, and which administrators also determined was not only not amusing but indicative of dangerous thinking: "Symbols or signs long associated with hate and violence towards specific groups for their religious beliefs, skin color, sexual orientation, or any aspect of difference, have the power to hurt and intimidate even when these are purportedly used in cartoon fun." In referring to my ad, the statement reluctantly conceded that my text might fall "within the realm of free speech and protected as a constitutional right," but warned:

> In protecting and asserting such a basic freedom, however, we must also note that with our freedoms come responsibility and choice. Freedom asserted without care and thought for others can become destructive to the community and our joint humanity.

---

66. Aaron Nathans, "Two Months Later, Bureaucrats at UW Criticize Ad in Herald," *Capital Times*, May 7, 2001.

The statement caught the *Herald* staff off guard. "For the university to drum up a response over two months later without saying anything to us was really surprising," Alex Conant told a *Capital Times* reporter. "For the administration to come down, not as individuals, but as the Dean of Students' Office, as the Office of Admissions, as the Wisconsin Union, to say we've gone too far in promoting that debate, that we're somehow inhibiting them from doing their job, is extremely heavy-handed."[67]

But Conant's remarks were mild compared to the stinging editorial rebuke that appeared four days later in the *Wisconsin State Journal*, the principal paper of the Madison community:

> The outrageous behavior of the week award goes to the 72 UW-Madison faculty and staff who condemned a campus newspaper for daring to expose students to a politically incorrect viewpoint. These university personnel have left UW-Madison Chancellor John Wiley with some work to do to repair the school's reputation as a place where the free exchange of ideas flourishes.[68]

The editorial was acerbic about the administrators' comment on my ad, saying, "The implication was clear: The *Badger Herald*'s editors made an irresponsible choice in printing Horowitz's views. UW-Madison welcomes all students—but not all ideas."

The usual script in academic affairs like this is for the heterodox students to be intimidated into silence or brought before some sort of kangaroo court proceeding, or to some point of public self-abasement. But the Wisconsin denouement proved to be different. The "offending" students actually felt strengthened by their experience, and reinforced in their ideas. It became one of those rare moments on today's campuses when an internal political event became a learning experience and a form, however unintended, of moral instruction.

Thus the most damning indictment was reserved to the students themselves. In the final issue of the *Herald*, which appeared on May 10, Hasdai Westbrook expressed the sentiments of the *Herald* staff.

> I thought I was graduating from college, not day care. According to a statement published in Monday's *Badger Herald*, a cabal of UW administrators apparently feels its job is to educate "faculty, staff and students on civil behavior towards one another, and on asserting our precious freedoms conscientiously." I disrespectfully disagree....

---

67. Ibid.
68. "Freedom of Thought Is in Danger at UW" (editorial), *Wisconsin State Journal*, 11 May 2001.

Civility is for dinner parties and fund-raisers, not the free press. Certainly it's always nice when people are nice to each other. But being nice is not a moral imperative and it certainly does not trump free expression.

Not according to the undersigned. Many of those who signed the statement are no doubt dedicated to helping students. One of them has given me invaluable aid with my academic affairs. But the administrators' pathetic, semi-official call for censorship displays nothing but political cowardice and a scary enthusiasm for treating college students like children.

Westbrook then turned his attention to the student protesters:

A small but vocal and well-connected percentage of students on this campus are demanding to be treated like children. They demand to be protected from ideas they hate and words that wound their emotions. They assert a right to not have their feelings hurt. To this end they have allied with more fanatical members of the administration to attack free speech.

Some examples: The dean of students' Speak Up program defines offensive speech as "verbal harassment," and pretends that it has the legal power to punish it. Student activists fought ardently to maintain the university's Orwellian faculty-speech code. And last semester, the administration, with behind-the-scenes funding and support from the U.S. Justice Department, tried to put up anonymous informant boxes in bathrooms for the collection of unverifiable harassment accusations. . . . It is sickening to watch administrators cower before politically correct fundamentalists. It is not the business of university administrators to concern themselves with the civility of debate outside the classroom. Or to take sides—apparently the administration is unconcerned about the civility of protestors who screamed offensive epithets at *Herald* staff members.

The authors of the statement wish to solve perceived campus-climate problems by telling the *Herald* to shut up. I have a better solution: People who cannot stand to hear opinions they disagree with should stop up their ears with cotton and lock themselves in a soundproof chamber with UW administrators. I'm sure things will be quite civil there.

Censorship and cowardice are not the values the University of Wisconsin should be promoting. A university is supposed to confirm us as adults by helping us to pursue knowledge. Instead, UW administrators wish to act as speech inquisitors, protecting us as children from the menace of other ideas.

My hat is off to Hasdai Westbrook and the editors of the *Badger Herald*. Our nation's press will be stronger and more principled if they should choose journalism as their life's work.

*Never could I have imagined an event that would so quickly lay
bare the tensions beneath Brown's surface. An event that proved
to the community, and to the world, just how intolerant the
supposed "liberal Ivy" really is.*
  Gregory Cooper, '01, *Brown Daily Herald,*
  May 28, 2001

FOUR

THE PROFESSORS (BROWN)

I n the Ivy League, Brown University has a reputation as a
school for high-class political celebrities and hard-line political correctness. Amy Carter and John F. Kennedy Jr. were
undergraduates there. But in the speech-code era of the 1990s,
the campus was also the venue for notoriously false sexual harassment
and rape cases that resulted in expensive court settlements and an embar-
rassing, high-visibility profile by John Stossel on ABC-TV's *20/20*. Below
the national radar, attacks on visiting conservatives were routine. When
Christian Coalition head Ralph Reed spoke at Brown, screaming protesters
shouted him down as a "racist," a "homophobe" and an "anti-Semite,"
making it impossible for anyone to hear him. The gay, feminist maverick
Camille Paglia called Brown "the most viciously intolerant campus I ever
visited as a lecturer."[69]
  The incidents at Berkeley and Wisconsin were exerting ripple effects
across the nation. Both campuses had just erupted when Joan Walsh's column, "Who's Afraid of the Big Bad Horowitz?" appeared in *Salon.* "The
Horowitz ad," Walsh wrote, "is explosive because for too many years
campuses have been places where ideological bullies, usually on the left,

---

69. Travis Rowley, "U. Must Reclaim Ability for Conservatives to Speak Freely," *Brown
Daily Herald,* 17 April 2001; Gregory Cooper, "Tumbling down the Rabbit Hole,"
Brown Daily Herald, 28 May 2001.

have been devoted to blocking political debate, rather than engaging it—and they've succeeded."[70] Coming from a writer with solid credentials on the left (and herself a former editor of the *Wisconsin Daily Cardinal*), this was a powerful defense of the intellectual marketplace. By this time the ad had been submitted to more than forty campus papers with only nine printing it.[71]

Brooks King, the editor of the *Brown Daily Herald*, read Joan Walsh's *Salon* story and phoned Alex Conant at the *Wisconsin Badger Herald* for advice. After taking his counsel, King concluded that the Brown paper should publish it if we approached them. He e-mailed the Walsh article to the other editors along with this advice.[72]

On Monday, March 12, the ad arrived and that evening the *Brown Daily Herald* editors decided to print it without comment. "We discussed it very briefly," Jahred Adelman recalls. "We thought it might upset some of our readers, but we also thought it's not our responsibility to censor this conservative opinion. Our decision was in keeping with the precedents of *Herald* advertising policy." The only serious question was whether the *Herald* should comment editorially. The idea was rejected because it was thought that doing so would set a difficult precedent requiring every ad that anyone thought controversial to be accompanied by a balancing commentary.[73] The ad appeared on Tuesday, March 13, under a banner that said "Paid Advertisement." The space cost $580.

This relatively small sum—a contrast to the $10,000 speaking fees casually paid out of student funds to Communists like Angela Davis and racists like Louis Farrakhan—was to become a major focus of the attacks that followed, which once again were directed far more at the paper that printed the ad than at the contents of the ad itself. Organizing these attacks was a Nigerian-American named Asmara Ghebremichael, a Brown senior and "Afro-American studies concentrator." A friend showed Ghebremichael the ad in a sociology class they were taking called "Intimate Violence." Ghebremichael went immediately to work organizing a Coalition of Concerned Brown Students to protest its appearance. By the following day she had two hundred signatures on a petition and eleven campus groups in support. These included the Black Student Union, Third World Action, the Brown Coalition for Social Justice, the Asian-American

---

70. Joan Walsh, "Who's Afraid of the Big Bad Horowitz?" *Salon.com,* 9 March 2001.
71. My office kept a running scorecard of these incidents at our website, www. frontpagemagazine.com, so that others—including the press—could see the story as it unfolded.
72. Norman Boucher, "The War over Words," *Brown Alumni Magazine,* May 2001.
73. Ibid.

Students Association and the campus chapters of the Young Communist League and the International Socialist Organization.[74]

The Coalition of Concerned Brown Students united behind two demands: first, that the money Brown had received in payment for the ad "be given back to the Brown minority community" in the form of a donation to the Third World Center; and second, that the *Daily Herald* provide a "free" page to the coalition "for the purpose of educating the greater Brown community on related issues and other issues important in the minority community in order to protect ourselves in the future from irrational publications like this one authored by David Horowitz."

The *Herald* editors rejected both demands, but agreed to print an op-ed piece by Ghebremichael, which appeared the next day, March 15. Titled "Free Speech Is Only for Those Who Can Afford to Pay," it made the left's case, but typically failed to answer any of the arguments of my ad.[75] The garbled syntax and gyrating diction of its prose suggested that Brown had failed at least part of its educational mission with respect to this graduating senior.

> *Brown Daily Herald* I assume you must be a little bewildered right now. I know you were scared when we called you asking how much you got paid for the ad entitled "Ten Reasons Why Reparations for Slavery Is a Bad Idea—and Racist Too." Whoops! I assume you didn't mean to be the test case for David Horowitz's campus fascism test,[76] but didn't you hear? There is a political war going on and you are the pawn of it.... For some reason the exchange of money makes everything okay. Dare us even to ask ourselves to distinguish between right and wrong. Naw, you all like to hide behind code words like "liberal" and "conservative" and the most nefarious of all, "paid advertisement."
>
> But (oh no!) the crisis of free speech! If we don't print the ad, (you must have thought) Ward Connolly [*sic*] might write a letter declaring how fascist our universities are.... There is a broader issue at hand here: Are you going to protect the free speech rights of the rich or the poor? Horowitz is saying that as long as you can back your words with money, anything goes: lies, harassment and hate included. He could have sent his commentary as a letter or a guest column, but no, he sent it as a paid advertisement. There was an exchange of money. Thus, the issue is not what was actually written, but the money that went into getting it printed.

---

74. "AASA Stands in Support of TWC's Demands of *Herald*," *Brown Daily Herald*, 15 March 2001.
75. *Brown Daily Herald*, 15 March 2001.
76. "Campus fascism" was a term I had used in interviews with the media to describe the attacks on me and my ad.

They are trying to get us mad so that we demand you recant the ad, and [then] they can scream and yell that free speech is being restricted (a.k.a. Vote Republican). But, you know what? We don't want you to recant the ad. We don't want an apology. What we do want is this, and we have 200 signatures to prove it. We want the money you accepted for running the ad to go to the Third World Center, and we want one free page of advertisement space to print whatever the hell we want to print.

Ghebremichael's column was not the end of the money issue, which kept resurfacing as a theme throughout the controversy. One reason was its deep roots in the ideology of the campus left. In his notorious essay "Repressive Tolerance," Marcuse had written: "The Left has no equal voice, no equal access to the mass media and their public facilities—not because a conspiracy excludes it, but because, in good old capitalist fashion, it does not have the required purchasing power."[77] Of course Ghebremichael and her comrades could have collected $3 apiece from the two hundred student signers of the petition and amassed the purchasing power to pay for an ad. But the issue refused to die.[78]

Asmara Ghebremichael's column did actually refer, in passing, to one of the arguments I had made: "What sort of integrity do you have," she asked the *Daily Herald,* "that you would actually print something that said, 'There was never an anti-slavery movement until white Anglo-Saxon Christians created one.'"[79] In fact, this was the entire extent of her comments on the ad except for the blanket charge that all the historical claims it made were fabricated for profit.[80]

---

77. Marcuse and Wolff, *A Critique of Pure Tolerance,* p. 119.
78. A subsequent *Herald* guest column by David Abramson, director of undergraduate studies at the Watson Institute for International Studies at Brown, had this programmatic (if ungrammatical) headline: "Money Provides Access to Media of 'Free Speech.'" The article showed how fashionable the Marcuse-Marxist model still was and how deep the animus against (and ignorance of) the American Founding: "What is … offensive is the awareness that the very Constitution that was once used to support the financing of slavery is now being used to legitimize claims that the relationship between economics and public speech is a disinterested one." *Brown Daily Herald,* 1 May 2001.
79. In an e-mail to supporters, Ghebremichael's coalition wrote, "We will not silently allow lies to be printed about our passivity in resisting slavery under the false auspices of protecting freedom of speech."
80. "We, as a community, are being harassed. Our history is being twisted and manipulated for the purpose of the profiteering of Horowitz (and on a smaller scale, the *Herald*)."

I probably could have formulated the point in question more carefully, since Ghebremichael was not alone in failing to understand it. But those who found it objectionable could also have made more of an effort to grasp what it was saying. Properly interpreted, the claim was not even controversial, which was a large part of the reason it hadn't occurred to me to elaborate it further. For thousands of years, until the end of the eighteenth century, slavery had been considered a normal institution of human societies. In all that time, no group had arisen to challenge its legitimacy. Of course, there were many slave revolts from the times of Moses and Sparatacus, in which those who had been enslaved sought to gain their freedom. But that was not the point. The freedom they had sought was their own. They did not revolt against the institution of slavery as such.

What had happened in the English-speaking countries at the dawn of the American Republic was entirely unique. Before then, no one had thought to form a movement dedicated to the belief that the institution of slavery was itself immoral. What was important in this historical fact was that it showed that white Europeans who were the target of the reparations indictment had played a pivotal role in the emancipation from slavery.

That it could be regarded as controversial (let alone outrageous) to say a debt is owed to the white Christians and American Founders who launched a movement to end slavery shows how bitter what passes for dialogue on race has become.[81] The scholarship on this issue is not the least ambiguous, as can be seen from this passage in an authoritative text on the subject by the Nobel-prizewinning historian Robert Fogel:

> The last quarter of the Seventeenth Century and the first three quarters of the Eighteenth Century were a watershed between the routine acceptance of slavery and the onset of a concerted, successful movement for the abolition of human bondage. . . . The moment at which

---

81. A typical example of the outrage can be found in the reply to the ad by Robert Chrisman and Ernest Allen Jr., "Ten Reasons: A Response to David Horowitz," www.umass.edu/afroam/hor.html. (This document was widely circulated by Afro-American Studies departments across the country.) "Horowitz's assertion that 'in the thousand years of slavery's existence, there never was an anti-slavery movement until white Anglo-Saxon Christians created one,' only demonstrates his ignorance concerning the formidable efforts of blacks to free themselves. Led by black Toussaint L'Overture, the Haitian revolution of 1793 overthrew the French slave system . . ." etc. The pair go on to mention several slave revolts (Gabriel Prosser, Denmark Vesey, Nat Turner) and abolitionist efforts, all of which postdated the creation of the anti-slavery movement by Christians in 1787. It was a common misperception of my ad that I slighted the efforts of African slaves to free themselves. I was defending those whites who had honorable anti-slavery sentiments and deeds to their credit against the claims of the reparations partisans. There was obviously no reason, in making such an argument, to comment on the efforts of blacks themselves.

abolitionism passed over from apparently ineffectual harangues by isolated zealots to a significant political movement cannot be dated with precision. Nevertheless, 1787, the year a handful of English Friends and evangelicals launched a public campaign against the slave trade, seems to be a reasonable, although not unique, occasion to mark the onset of concerted political action to end slavery. Slavery was abolished in its last American bastion—Brazil—in 1888. And so, within the span of a little more than a century, *a system that had stood above criticism for 3,000 years was outlawed everywhere in the Western world.*[82] [emphasis added]

Every professor of American history within range of the ad who knew anything about slavery—and there were surely hundreds of them—knew precisely what I was referring to, and knew that the point I had made in the ad was historically accurate. But *not one* of them came forward to defend it. Instead they allowed black students, like Asmara Ghebremichael, to remain comfortable in their ignorance of facts that should have been regarded as central to the understanding of their own history. That was what the specter of fear that now haunts our campuses had accomplished.

The evening Ghebremichael's column appeared, Brooks King and members of the *Brown Daily Herald* editorial board sat down to discuss matters with the radical coalition. "We declined to meet their demands right off the bat," King said later. "Things went downhill from there." Before the meeting dissolved, one member of the coalition said: "If you don't give in to our demands ... no one's going to read your papers. We're going to ensure that your papers aren't read on campus."[83]

The next morning was Friday, and the Coalition of Concerned Brown Students made good on its threat. Its members fanned out across the campus and stole the entire edition of the *Daily Herald*—nearly four thousand copies—from the distribution points.[84] In place of the missing papers the coalition left pink and orange fliers explaining their rationale for the theft: "It is the profits gained from publishing Horowitz's ad that incited our action." The flier continued: "Members of the Coalition do not regret the necessary removal of the papers in protest and self-defense. The *Herald*'s

---

82. Robert William Fogel, *Without Consent or Contract: The Rise and Fall of American Slavery* (New York, 1989), p. 205.
83. Boucher, "The War over Words."
84. "The coalition took all the copies of the *Herald* from more than ten locations, leaving the campus with almost no copies of the newspaper. Only the news rack at the *Herald* offices remained full, despite two attempts by coalition members to take the copies in the rack." Andy Golodny, "Coalition Seizes Nearly 4,000 Copies of Herald," *Brown Daily Herald*, 16 March 2001.

decision to run the ad ... was a direct assault on communities of color and their allies at Brown." Then, in a perfect Orwellian flourish, the vandals also proclaimed: "The Coalition has never opposed free speech."[85]

The theft was a front-page story in the *Boston Globe* and, over the next few days, also made the front page of the *New York Times* and was picked up by the *Washington Post,* ABC News and the BBC. On Sunday, Brooks King went on NBC's *Weekend Today* to debate a former *Brown Daily Herald* columnist and member of the International Socialist Organization—a Trotskyist sect and pillar of the student coalition—who had resigned his position on the *Herald* staff to protest the ad.[86]

The *Daily Herald* staff responded to the vandalism by reprinting one thousand copies of the stolen issue and hand-distributing it to students on Saturday in the "Ratty," the Student Union and dining area. Brooks King described the theft as "an action meant to intimidate and frighten," and the editors announced they would pursue criminal charges against the culprits. They condemned the act as "an unacceptable attempt to silence our voice." The president of the campus ACLU, a junior named Carl Takei, was equally blunt: "This is the worst possible thing the coalition could have done, both to themselves and to free discourse at the University."

It proved to be a defining event for the Brown community. The next day, the university president, Sheila Blumstein, issued a formal statement:

> Consistent with its commitment to the free exchange of ideas, the University recognizes and supports the *Herald*'s right to publish any material it chooses, even if that material is objectionable to members of the campus community. The Office of Student Life will review information concerning these incidents.[87]

The coalition leaders now found themselves on the defensive, and were forced to argue extravagantly that their theft was an act of "civil disobedience." For help they turned to their faculty mentor, Professor Lewis R. Gordon, head of the Afro-American Studies Department and author of books on "black philosophy" and "African existentialism."[88] He was a member of the Radical Philosophy Association and had written several articles for *Political Affairs,* a journal that describes itself as the "theoretical organ of the American Communist Party." Gordon's most recent book, *Existentia Africana,* was dedicated to his mentor, Professor William

---

85. Andy Golodny, "Amid Ongoing Protests, U. Backs off Criticism of Herald Theft," *Brown Daily Herald,* 21 March 2001.

86. *Brown Daily Herald,* 21 March 2001; Boucher, "The War over Words."

87. *Brown Daily Herald,* 21 March 2001.

88. Lewis R. Gordon, *Existentia Africana* (New York, 2000), p. ix.

R. Jones, author of a treatise called *Is God a White Racist? A Preamble to Black Theology*. In the preface to *Existentia Africana,* Gordon describes Jones' work as a text in which "black liberation thinkers [are challenged] to take seriously the possibility that the signs and symbols of the Western religions upon which they depended may harbor the seeds of their destruction."

Asmara Ghebremichael and her fellow coalition leaders were feeling inadequate to answer the droves of television reporters descending on Brown. They asked Gordon to take over representing their case to the reporters.

When classes resumed on Monday, campus police officers and *Herald* staff members stood guard over news racks containing the new edition. When interviewed by reporter Andy Golodny, Professor Gordon took an aggressive if somewhat incoherent posture in explaining the students' actions: "If something is free, you can take as many copies as you like. This is not a free speech issue. It is a hate speech issue." Gordon was seconded by Kenneth Knies, a teaching assistant in his Afro-American Studies Department, who said: "I have talked to students who told me that they can't perform basic functions like walking or sleeping because of this ad."[89]

As a result of the theft and the passions it inflamed, the offices of the *Herald* and the Afro-American Studies Department became targets of hostile phone messages and e-mail flames. Anonymous callers to the *Herald* would say, "You're a racist" or "the *Brown Daily Herald* is racist," and then hang up.[90] Some of the e-mails were sent by anonymous off-campus visitors to the *Herald* website, others by angry students. The *Herald* editors attempted to brush them off.

Similar e-mails from the other side were not treated merely as ugly annoyances or measures of how high feelings were running. In the hands of Professor Gordon and his supporters, ventilations of outrage at the activists' antics were regarded as racial harassment, a sign that Brown was "unwelcoming" to all minorities, and a bloody flag to wave at every turn of the battle.

> Hello. Is this the asshole that ripped off all those papers because of that slavery article? What a bunch of chicken shit, bullshit. I mean, you're proving that you're inferior. You're proving it more and more

89. Andy Golodny, "Protesters Speak Out against Herald at Distribution Sites," *Brown Daily Herald,* 20 March 2001.
90. Shannon Tan, "Note Heightens Racial Tensions at Brown," *Boston Globe,* 24 March 2001.

all the time. And wait 'til you get out in the real fucking world. You'll find out really how useless you are....

A second message apparently left by the same caller used the word "nigger" in unambiguous hate speech. Two members of the coalition were sent a letter containing a photograph of African children with war wounds. "Reparations?" the letter writer asked. "You've got to be kidding!! Keep dreaming—something for nothing *again!!* ... You are *blessed* in *this* country! These children could be you!!"[91]

Gordon and his followers lost no time in laying responsibility for these incidents at the door of the *Herald* and the ad I had written. Under their pressure, President Blumstein shifted gears. Four days after she had condemned the coalition's theft of the papers, she issued a second statement now ascribing the problems to me: "Even as we uphold our principles, we cannot deny the impact the publication of this advertisement has had on the Brown community as a whole. It was written to be inflammatory. In addition, it was deliberately and deeply hurtful."[92]

Blumstein didn't specify how the ad was deliberately, let alone deeply hurtful. Nor did she attempt to justify her accusation that the ad was intentionally inflammatory. It could be so interpreted only if its text was deliberately or unwittingly misread. For example, Charles Bakst, a former editor of the *Herald* and now a political columnist for the *Providence Journal-Bulletin,* called the ad "an insult to anyone's intelligence" and described it as "bizarre and brazen," bidding his readers to "mull this assertion about the 'debt' blacks 'owe' to America." Then he contemptuously quoted my words: "If not for the sacrifices of white soldiers and a white American president who gave his life to sign the Emancipation Proclamation, blacks in America would still be slaves."[93]

The sentence I wrote is "bizarre" only if one thinks of whites in racist terms—that is, if one regards all whites as having enslaved blacks and none as having fought to free them. If one thinks in these terms, then freeing black slaves would be undoing a crime you yourself are responsible for (which is what many of my critics argued). Who should be grateful for that? But to make Lincoln and the Union soldiers responsible for the slave system they inherited and then destroyed, as Bakst and many outraged by the ad invariably did, was itself to distort history and twist the facts.

91. Boucher, "The War over Words."
92. Golodny, "Amid Ongoing Protests ... ," *Brown Daily Herald,* 21 March 2001.
93. M. Charles Bakst, "Brown Herald: Standing Up for Free Press," *Providence Journal-Bulletin,* 20 March 2001.

In an attempt to resolve the conflict, Brown president Blumstein organized several meetings between the sides. The first brought leaders of the coalition together with members of the student government, *Herald* editors and various deans. Lewis R. Gordon was the only professor invited. One of the *Herald* editors present, Patrick Moos, summed up the result: "We thought we were coming in to sit down and talk rationally, but the conversation was very one-sided. All the administrators—including people I really respect—were acting like we were clearly in the wrong. No one stood up for us."[94]

A subsequent panel of professors who discussed the issues before five hundred students[95] proved no more productive. Five of the six professors opposed the *Herald*'s stance. The *Herald* assigned a Brown sophomore named Alex Schulman to cover the event. Schulman wrote: "Many at Brown, and in America, agree with Horowitz in some, many or even all of his assertions. What about the marginalization of these people? What about the implied idea that they too are racists and somehow share responsibility in the hurt of the Brown community?"[96]

One panel member, a professor in the Afro-American Studies Department named James Campbell, went so far as to attack *Herald* editor Brooks King personally, calling him a "cynical opportunist." Alex Schulman thought this reflected the double standard at work among the professoriate. "Are we expected to believe that it is intrinsically horrific for a student of color to read Horowitz's ad, but somehow okay for a respected professor to tell a gathering of Brown students that their peer and hardworking editor in chief is a cynical opportunist?"

Professor Gordon was also on the panel and "resisted no opportunity to narrate stories of racist telephone messages at his office." But, Schulman observed, "there was virtually no mention of the extensive threats that *Herald* editors and supporters have endured since the ad ran in print." The *Herald* staffers were students, too. Maybe they were not black,[97] "but if words hurt, they hurt everyone."

Although the campus adults were putting enormous pressure on the *Herald,* the students were not giving in. To oppose the coalition, Carl Takei

---

94. Boucher, "The War over Words."
95. *Boston Globe,* 24 March 2001.
96. Alex Schulman, "Life after Horowitz," *Brown Daily Herald,* 5 April 2001.
97. The lack of blacks on the *Herald* staff was a recurring issue for the leftists as well. However, there was an active boycott of the *Herald* by the black left at Brown, which made recruitment impossible. According to the account of events in the *Brown Alumni Magazine,* which was highly sympathetic to the left's position in the dispute, the *Herald* had made serious efforts to recruit black staffers only to be rebuffed. Boucher, "The War over Words."

(head of the Brown ACLU) and other students took a page out of the play-book of the campus left and created an organization called Students of Color against Censorship. Takei was especially concerned about admin-istration members who had agreed with the coalition's claim that the ad was a "racial assault and a form of hate speech." He sent the following e-mail to Blumstein: "A number of individuals on this campus have described the Horowitz ad as being 'hate speech' or a 'hate assault,' in an attempt to justify the Coalition's claims that this is not a free speech issue. The Horowitz ad is clearly a political advocacy piece." Takei asked Blumstein to "send a clear message to your senior administrators that the Horowitz ad is not an example of hate speech."[98]

At a faculty meeting called by Blumstein to discuss the issue, physics professor Philip Bray expressed his dismay at the attack on the paper. "I am concerned that some students insist that taking the *Brown Daily Her-ald* is not thievery," he said. "Those papers were stolen from thousands of students, staff and faculty, and that is theft." There was audible sup-port for Bray's views from some of the faculty attending. Then Lewis Gor-don rose to speak. "It is utter insensitivity to leap to certain conclusions about acts of civil disobedience. You can say 'hear hear,' but I find it grotesquely hypocritical."[99]

While Bray and other supporters of the *Herald* remained isolated and unorganized, Lewis Gordon was busily rallying the faculty left. On April 4, the *Herald* leaked a private letter to President Blumstein, which was eventually published over the signatures of sixty Brown professors. The faculty signers were "angered and saddened by the lack of leadership" the university had shown, and saw it as an attack on Brown's minorities: "Your refusal to condemn the advertisement as a form of harassment has—perhaps inadvertently—led to the silencing of many people of color on campus." Even worse was the university's effort to inquire whether the theft had involved a violation of university rules. The professors were out-raged: "A few students of color have been egregiously selected by the admin-istration as scapegoats for an investigation of violations of Brown's stu-dent code of conduct." Rather than a theft, they argued, the removal of the papers was a "symbolic protest over both the publication of Horowitz's commercial ad, and the *Brown Daily Herald*'s refusal to provide the stu-dents with equal space, free of charge, for a response to the ad's racist and assaultive statements."

---

98. Golodny, "Amid Ongoing Protests . . ."
99. Ibid.

The statement continued: "Faculty and staff of color on campus, together with their white supporters, increasingly feel genuinely harassed and unwelcome at this institution," and called for an investigation of the e-mail flamers:

> As you know, the University can use IP addresses to trace the source of every communication, anonymous or otherwise, on the web.... Rather than actively investigating those who have been posting anonymous threats and racial slurs online, which have assaulted and silenced Brown's community of people of color, the University has chosen to investigate a few students who took part in this symbolic act. We find this misplaced investigation shocking.... Surely, the University has a greater responsibility to its faculty, staff and students of color to "investigate" those who are publishing such injurious comments, than it does to scapegoat a few students for what was clearly an action undertaken collectively as a symbolic protest against a blatantly racist advertisement that went unchallenged by the University.[100]

The faculty statement drew a response from a handful of brave professors. Whereas the sixty signers of the letter were drawn from departments that taught history, political science and African-American studies, the opposition came exclusively from departments where political correctness was not part of the hiring or teaching process: the medical school, and the music and biology departments. The most pointed remarks were contained in a letter to the editor of the *Herald* by Professor Kenneth R. Miller, author of *Finding Darwin's God: A Scientist's Search for Common Ground between God and Evolution*.[101] The situation at Brown, he wrote, could be "a classic study of how political tyrannies develop." He urged Blumstein to make this an object lesson for students. "Ideologies of both the right and left take control of free societies by taking a legitimate concern or grievance, claiming that the institutions of a free society are not sufficient to deal with it and then installing themselves in positions of absolute control and authority." Miller pointed to the McCarthy Fifties as a time when lives, careers and institutions were destroyed by crusaders of the right in their zeal to protect the country against Communism. He then drew a parallel to the situation at Brown:

> The faculty who signed that letter have, just like McCarthy, taken a legitimate issue—the fear of racism—as their own.... In [their letter]

---

100. "Complete Text of Faculty Letter to President Blumstein," *Brown Daily Herald*, 12 April 2001.
101. Kenneth R. Miller, "Faculty Letter Threatens Sanctity of Free Speech at Brown," *Brown Daily Herald*, 12 April 2001.

they asked you to condemn the Horowitz advertisement as a form of "harassment," a remarkable request showing how thoroughly they have confused words with deeds. Not surprisingly, their [letter] also refers to an act of petty theft as "symbolic action" and asks the University to investigate newspaper writers who have "viciously slandered" Brown faculty members. They'd be pleased, no doubt, if you formed a standing "Un-Brunonian Activities Committee" to police speech and thought among students and faculty—all in the name of protecting us against racism.

The nature and extent of actual racism at Brown remained shadowy and subjective. The letter from the sixty faculty members produced none of the alleged "threats" to themselves or to the campus minorities. But it did provide an appendix with "examples of hate speech from the *Brown Daily Herald*'s online forums." The e-mail flames were revealing, but not in the way the professors intended:

- Perhaps we should call them "Third World ingrates" or better yet crybabies. They are humiliating our school, and diminishing the value of our diplomas. That such moronic students should be permitted to step through the Van Winkle gates is the real crime. How on earth were they accepted in the first place? Perhaps affirmative action had a TINY bit to do with it?
- I am offended by the term used in the article "People of Color." This is a racist term used to exclude only White people. . . .
- Or maybe you are a product of affirmative action, which would explain your limited ability to rationalize. I feel sorry for Brown because they have obviously lowered their standards for admission. That would explain the Third World Center membership and their inability to deal with opposing viewpoints in an adult manner.
- Well—if I, a White Non-Jewish male, stole some periodicals, which I had a "racial" problem with, I would be charged with a "HATE CRIME." If a "person of color" says "nigger," that's OK. But if I call a nigger a nigger—Whoah . . . There's a problem. I'm so fed up with all of this "you owe me for slavery." I don't own a nigger and wouldn't want one in my house. SO GET A LIFE or go back to the "Africa" that you all want the title of.

The use of the N-word has acquired totemic significance in environments like Brown, becoming, like *Yaweh*, a word that is forbidden for the orthodox to utter or hear. But while the e-mails reflected some callow undergraduate attitudes and some genuine resentment, they were hardly evidence of a racial terror at Brown.

■   ■

I had been invited by the College Republicans to speak at Brown in the beginning of April, and was scheduled to go there after three speaking engagements that had been already set for me in the Boston area.[102] But just prior to my departure, Todd Auwater, head of the Brown Republicans, contacted my office. He said the invitation was being withdrawn because the left was threatening violence if I came.[103]

The College Republicans had planned the event as a public debate. A self-described "liberal Republican," Auwater told a reporter his rationale for organizing the event: "[Republicans] believed that by getting these arguments out in the open, the Brown community would come to a deeper understanding of the issues."[104] Auwater invited Lewis Gordon to debate me. Gordon declined, invoking the baroque and not particularly convincing excuse that "it would be irresponsible for me to do so since my position on black reparations is that it is too narrowly defined as an issue." The head of the Providence NAACP accepted in his stead and the Brown administration reluctantly went along with idea. Laura Fried, Brown's executive vice president for public affairs, commented: "I think Horowitz's brand of free speech is noxious, but students have the right to bring whomever they want onto campus as long as they make the proper arrangements."[105]

After I accepted the invitation, Auwater was visited by Josh Segall, a former president of the College Democrats. He was accompanied by the representative of a Marxist sect called the Student Labor Alliance, and by the member of the International Socialists who had resigned from the *Brown Daily Herald* over my ad. According to Auwater, "They told me that Horowitz's presence would result in violent protests. They were concerned that the emotional state of the campus was so fragile that having a debate at this time would result in unpleasant things happening." Auwater did not want violence and rescinded the invitation. The Brown administration conducted no investigations of the threat.

An intriguing footnote to the incident was buried in the *Providence Journal-Bulletin* story. When talking to Auwater, "Segall said he heard that several students burst into tears when they heard that Horowitz might be coming to campus." Apparently victimhood is a campus art form at Brown.

---

102. At the University of Massachusetts, Boston University and MIT.
103. See "Fearing Violence, Republicans Withdraw Invitation to Horowitz," *Brown Daily Herald,* 2 April 2001.
104. "Student Group Cancels Horowitz Talk at Brown," *Providence Journal-Bulletin,* 3 April 2001.
105. Ibid.

But while I was being denied a platform, the campus left was able to arrange a speaking engagement for Sam Anderson, a self-styled founder of the Harlem branch of the Black Panther Party—and to finance his visit. Anderson told a packed audience in Brown's MacMillan Hall, "The people here who have taken up the struggle against a man named 'Horroritz' have done a great thing."[106] He spoke about the larger struggle against "white supremacy" and the "eradication of its material basis," which was "capitalism." Cuba, he said, was a good example of a country that had eliminated capitalism. He warned his audience "the struggle is not a nice struggle.... The enemy is not nice."

During the question period, a white audience member asked the Panther to clarify who this enemy was. "Am I the enemy because I am white?" Anderson didn't blink. "The enemy I'm talking about is predominantly the white class and their Negro lackeys," he said.

Another event the left arranged was a forum on April 7 that featured Lewis Gordon and Nation of Islam spokesman Brother Everett Muhammad. About an hour into the meeting, "one senior upset that many black students didn't know the facts they'd need to rebut Horowitz, condemned Brown as a racist institution with no interest in African-Americans."[107]

It was a telling point. The black students had been shunted to the background in the battle. At its outset Asmara Ghebremichael had thrown down a gauntlet. "We don't want an apology," she had written in her original *Herald* column. "What we do want is... one free page of advertisement space to print... an article on reparations. This one won't be full of propaganda and lies however."[108]

The article never appeared. During the entire controversy, the students objecting to the ad had not been able to produce their promised rebuttal. Neither had the entire faculty of the Afro-American Studies Department at Brown.

Lewis Gordon's presence on the panel made the moment particularly tense. After listening to the student's complaint, the professor sprang to the defense of the institution that was paying him a six-figure income, and launched into an attack on the black students present who until this moment had depended on him. As the *Providence Journal-Bulletin* reported, "Professor Lewis Gordon, who is head of Africana studies and has rallied

---

106. "Black Panthers Branch Founder Speaks on Need for Reparations," *Brown Daily Herald,* 17 April 2001.
107. Marion Davis, "Anger at Brown Still Simmers over Divisive Ad," *Providence Journal-Bulletin,* 8 April 2001.
108. "Free Speech Is Only for Those Who Can Afford to Pay."

support for the coalition among the faculty, chided the senior for her 'very sweeping' statements, noting, 'I'm Brown University, too.' Black people at Brown have taken 'a lot of heat' over the years to make the university what it is, Gordon said, and the students' 'politically immature' actions and 'anti-intellectualism' are damaging to all." Gordon then warned the black students in the audience against further divisive complaints.[109]

Brother Everett Muhammad, the black Muslim, who was not beholden to Brown, came to the student's defense. "Muhammad expressed anger about the tone of Gordon's admonitions, and they argued loudly. A student started crying and shouted, 'Why are black people arguing with each other?'"

At this point, Gordon exited the hall, and a black studies professor from Roger Williams University took the microphone to defend the young activists: "I think these students, being a minority... being aware of that issue, constantly makes you feel very isolated." It was another moment of blame, another passing of the buck. Misguided by their faculty advisers, and by a political tradition that instructed them to regard themselves only as victims and to seek confrontation with the rest of the world, these students had worked themselves into a painful corner, and none of their mentors was going to show them a way out.

109. Davis, "Anger at Brown Still Simmers."

Treason to whiteness is loyalty to humanity.
Professor Noel Ignatiev

FIVE

TRADUCING HISTORY

n April 4, I went to MIT for a debate with Dorothy Benton-Lewis, head of the National Coalition for Reparations against Blacks. The proceedings were broadcast on C-Span and took place before a well-behaved audience of three hundred MIT students and more than a dozen campus security guards. The unusual calm of the audience started me thinking that maybe these precautions were superfluous. But when it was over, and my security team had whisked me off the stage and through an underground passage to a waiting car in the back, a deranged white woman suddenly appeared and came at me screaming. She had sat through the debate, making bizarre gestures that my guard noticed (but I did not), and had somehow managed to run out, locate us, and break through the security perimeter MIT had provided. The incident persuaded me, if I needed persuading, that anyone bringing politically incorrect views about race onto campus ought to think about bringing a bodyguard too.

The invitation to MIT had come from a black fraternity, Alpha Phi Alpha, whose president, Jonathan White, was solicitous and respectful, the very model of the civility that had been noticeably absent in all these events. I was introduced by another member of Alpha Phi Alpha, Christopher D. Smith, who was equally courteous and told me he had recently been hired as an engineer with a large Boston-area firm. In an interview with the campus paper White said he regarded reparations as a "complex issue," but supported the idea of doing something for black Americans though not necessarily "in monetary form." Smith told the same reporter: "I am actually strongly opposed to reparations. As a black person living in 2001, I find the whole idea of reparations to be inappropriate."[110]

When the debate began, we were once again transported to a realm of the surreal. At one point, Dorothy Benton-Lewis said: "Anytime you have to depend on the country that enslaved you, to feed, clothe and shelter you, you are still a slave. There were 4 million slaves at the end of emancipation. We still have 2 million slaves in American prisons; they are our concentration camps. We are still enslaved; we are just modern-day slaves."[111] I looked out into the audience of well-dressed MIT students who could expect to earn $70,000 a year or more upon graduation, about a third of whom were black, and said: "I don't see any slaves here."

On my way to the debate, I had passed a bulletin board of notices of other events taking place at the college. When I glanced over the announcements, I saw that one of them publicized a lecture that had been given the day before by Professor Noel Ignatiev. The name was familiar to me and so was the subject of the talk: "The Way Forward: Abolish the White Race."[112] What struck me about the announcement, which was formally printed and officially presented by the MIT events office, was the fact that despite its inflammatory message, there had been no campus protests, nor would there be any over the many presentations just like it that take place at MIT and other campuses almost every day of the academic year. Unlike my critique of reparations, Ignatiev's perspective was a familiar one to the academy. The title of the talk reflected the central paradigm of "Whiteness Studies," one of the fastest-growing fields in the liberal arts curriculum, of which Ignatiev was a leading exponent. Ignatiev was the editor of a magazine called *Race Traitor,* whose well-known motto was "Treason to Whiteness Is Loyalty to Humanity." His anti-white views were shared by proponents of other academic trends like "Critical Race Studies," which was a powerful presence in law schools across the country.[113]

---

110. A. S. Wang and Dana Levine, "Horowitz, Benton-Lewis Debate," *The Tech,* 6 April 2001.
111. MIT debate, http://video.C-span.org:8080/ramgen/ndrive/e040701_slavery.rm.
112. MIT Calendar, Tuesday, April 3, 2001, 4:30–6:00 P.M., Rm. 14E-304.
113. A book of selections from Ignatiev's magazine has been published by a major academic publisher under the same title, *Race Traitor* (New York, 1996). See especially the editorial in this volume by Ignatiev and John Garvey, "Abolish the White Race by Any Means Necessary," pp. 90–114. Ignatiev's perspectives fall within the framework of a leftist ideology that pervades Afro-American Studies and other "interdisciplinary" fields of the liberal arts curriculum, including "Cultural Studies," "American Studies" and "Critical Race Studies," all of these manifestations of a school of academics who promote extreme racialist doctrines. Among the influential texts of

Ignatiev's talk on abolishing the white race had been sponsored by two official bodies at MIT—the Committee on Campus Race Relations and the Program in Writing and Humanistic Studies. Obviously the campus authorities did not consider this proposal to "abolish" them as "insensitive" to white students or feel that it might damage a "welcoming environment" for them.

For Ignatiev and his professorial colleagues, "whiteness" was the organizing principle of American society and the main instrument of its oppressive relationship to ethnic minorities. It is easy to see how the reparations movement, with its loose application of the term "racist" and its promiscuous use of the slavery metaphor, fit this academic model. The slavery metaphor is already present in Marxist theories which have shaped academic radicalism, and which characterize free-market workers as "wage-slaves." Tenured leftists like Ignatiev have simply replaced Marx's "class war," in their conceptual framework, with the idea of race war.[114]

Michael Eric Dyson, a black professor at DePaul University active in the reparations campaign (and eventually one of my antagonists) put these intellectual concepts together in a characteristic effusion for an academic anthology called *White Reign.* He explained that racism and slavery are, in fact, America's essence:

> Whiteness as domination has been the most powerful, sustaining myth of American culture since its inception. In other words, the ideological contamination of American democracy by structures of white domination is indivisible from the invention of America....
>
> The expansion of American culture, especially the American State, was fostered primarily through the labor of black slaves and, to a lesser degree, the exploitation of white indentured servants and the oppression of white females. From the very beginning of our nation's existence, the discursive defense and political logic of American democracy has spawned white dominance as the foundational myth of American society.[115]

---

the expansive literature already produced by the "whiteness studies" group are David Roediger, *Towards the Abolition of Whiteness* (New York, 1994), and George Lipsitz, *The Possessive Investment in Whiteness* (Philadelphia, 1984). "Critical Race Studies" is discussed by Daniel Farber and Suzanna Sherry in *Beyond All Reason: The Radical Assault on Truth in American Law* (New York, 1997).

114. Cf. Richard Delgado, *The Coming Race War* (New York, 1996). Delgado is a professor of law at the University of Colorado and an influential exponent of "critical race theory."

115. Michael Eric Dyson, "Giving Whiteness a Black Eye," in *White Reign: Deploying Whiteness in America,* ed. Kincheloe et al. (New York, 1998), p. 301.

However bizarre their ideas, figures like Ignatiev and Dyson are not controversial on campuses today. They are the academic equivalent of business as usual.

■   ■

Nothing in the ad had enraged my campus critics more than points 9 and 10, which observed that contemporary African-Americans are the wealthiest and freest community of black people in the world and thus the beneficiaries of American democracy. I suggested that like all citizens they owed a debt to the Americans who created the framework of freedom and opportunity from which they benefited. This recognition seemed to me essential for blacks themselves. How could one feel at home in a country if one's entire experience of it was viewed in negative terms? The struggle for freedom was a common heritage for both blacks and whites. That was the historical reality, and it had the potential to form a common bond uniting both races in the already existing American community. It was this idea, in particular, that was anathema to my opponents.

While these points seemed self-evident to me, however, they provoked a storm of abuse. I was accused (by *Chicago Tribune* columnist Clarence Page) of suggesting that "those slave shackles were lined with gold."[116] My argument was likened to a statement that a rape victim should be grateful to her rapist if he buys her a dress afterwards.[117] Two black scholars wrote in their response: "Please excuse the analogy, but if someone

---

116. Clarence Page, "Race Baiting for Fame and Profit," *Chicago Tribune*, 26 March 2001. I sent a note to Page in reply to his attack: "My comment about the comparative wealth of African-Americans and African natives was not designed, as you know, to belittle the economic deprivation and poverty of blacks living in America or to suggest that America has made all blacks rich. It was an answer to Randall Robinson and his fellow reparations proponents, who argue that only non-blacks have benefited from the post-slavery economy of the United States. It was a way of saying it's time to celebrate African-American success in the New World. Even if you did not read point 10 of my ad carefully, you are in a better position than most (since you know me) to realize that my intention here was to criticize a leadership that dwells on the negative, emphasizes failure, directs the attention of its constituency to the past rather than the future and—for those reasons—is not in my view serving African-Americans or the rest of America's ethnic communities well. This is a political criticism not a racial one." In all fairness to Clarence, he may not have been responsible for the offensive headline to his story, which, under editorial policy is often written by someone else.

117. "Even if your claim of a 'benefit' is true in some long-term narrative sense—like saying that a Thai girl who is raped by an American, brought to this country, and given a nice wardrobe benefited from her rape—your ascription of the benefit to the crime is, at a minimum, analytically wrong and morally obtuse." William Saletan, "White Whine," *Slate.com*, Wednesday, 28 March 2001.

chops off your fingers and then hands them back to you, should you be 'grateful' for having received your mangled fingers, or enraged that they were chopped off in the first place?"[118]

These were actually typical comments.[119] After I spoke at UC Santa Barbara, one agitated (white) undergraduate wrote:

> It is points 9 and 10 where Horowitz decides to burn a metaphorical cross and become the *crème de la crème* of racists. Here Horowitz claims that black people should be ever so thankful to whites.... For those of you too immersed in privilege to realize what this means, here is an example: You own a car. A complete stranger steals your car and runs it into the ground. When the car thief is done with the car he decides to give it back to you. Do you really feel like you should thank this car thief?... What is most striking about this is that it asks blacks to be thankful for a heritage of lynch mobs and slavery. As a Jew, I suppose Horowitz would like me to be thankful for the Nazi Holocaust. After all, if it hadn't been for mass genocide, my grandparents would not be refugees and I wouldn't be privileged to go to UCSB.[120]

The writer was blind not only to the text I had written, but also to the idea of historical progress. The theft of a car in a society that already regards theft as criminal is one thing; the practice of slavery in a world in which societies that are both black and white, both European and African regard it as a normative and legal institution, is quite another. No one suggested that freed slaves should be grateful to their slave-masters. The argument I made referred to blacks who were never slaves and to whites who were *not* slave owners and whose ancestors mostly had no connection to slavery or had fought to end it. The idea that slavery—as an institution— is wrong, as already noted, is an Anglo-American idea. America is the first predominantly white society to free its black slaves, and it did so long before black societies freed *theirs*. This is the history that needs recognition. But on American college campuses, that recognition comes at a high price for anyone who attempts to express it.

---

118. Chrisman and Allen, "Ten Reasons: A Response to David Horowitz."
119. Another example is the following, from a letter written by a senior to the campus paper at Duke (2 April 2001): "[Horowitz says] 'American blacks on average enjoy per capita incomes in the range of twenty to fifty times that of blacks living in any of the African nations from which they were kidnapped.' To blacks, this statement could easily read, 'We could take away your civil rights and half your money, and you would still be better off than those blacks left behind in Africa.'" My answer: It *could?*
120. Adam Kaiserman, "The Bigotry, Misconceptions, Behind the Ten Points," *UCSB Daily Nexus*, 1 June 2001.

On March 20, a week after the copies of the *Brown Daily Herald* were stolen, the student paper at Duke University published the ad. That same day, an angry delegation led by the Black Student Alliance marched into the editorial offices of the *Duke Chronicle*, claiming the ad had attacked their "identity" and their "political beliefs." A set of not very consistent demands was presented to the paper—to provide "two free pages" for a public apology and rebuttal, but also to contribute the $793.80 received from me for the ad to pay for their free ads' cost.

The protesters further demanded that the *Chronicle* provide adequate coverage of minority issues and institute a system of review for advertising decisions. The *Chronicle* editors defended their coverage and said that a policy for advertising already existed and that the ad itself had been extensively reviewed and the decision to publish it had been unanimous. Campus police were called in to remove the protesters when they refused to leave.[121]

A demonstration ensued. "The protesters marched around the main residential and academic quadrangles, chanting and waving signs. With intense anger and volume, the students began shouting 'We are students, too! Respect us, too!' and moved on to phrases such as 'Don't read the *Chronicle!*' 'It's all lies!' And 'I am not three-fifths of a student!' "[122]

The protesters also demanded that the Duke administration remove its financial support from the *Chronicle* by withdrawing any advertisements it had placed in the paper, and to issue a progress report on outstanding demands made by black students going back to 1969, when the campus administration building had been stormed. Among these demands were that the university create a segregated black student dormitory and a separate black student union paid for out of black student fees.[123]

These demands were presented to Duke president Nan Keohane during a silent vigil of mostly black students, many in tears, who formed a human chain one hundred strong in front of her offices. Keohane mostly listened to the complaints, then tried to reason with the protesters on the issue of free speech: "You may be overstating the extent to which free

---

121. Ambika Kumar, "Community Members Protest *Chronicle* Ad," *Duke Chronicle*, 22 March 2001; see also Kumar, "Ad Protesters Submit Demands, Get Responses," *Duke Chronicle*, 23 March 2001.

122. Ambika Kumar, "Students Hold Rally, Organize Monday Boycott," *Duke Chronicle*, 26 March 2001.

123. These two demands were rejected by Duke president Nan Keohane, who explained: "These propositions run counter to Duke's desire to build a community in which the recognition of diversity serves to educate all of us, not divide people from one another." "Keohane Issues Report on Racial Issues at Duke," www.dukenews.duke.edu/daily00-01/ report.htm.

speech can be protected from being hurtful and offensive," Keohane said to one of those present. "Free speech is not costless . . . it's hard to say there are things that just shouldn't be said."[124]

Keohane agreed to issue the report on previous demands that had not been met, but rejected the proposed boycott of the *Chronicle*. In an e-mail to two of the student leaders, she said: "The role of a great university is not to prohibit speech but to provide a forum where people can challenge falsehoods and debate issues on campuses and in our society."[125] Keohane also offered university funds to pay for space for a rebuttal of the ad in the *Chronicle*. But, as in previous cases, the rebuttal was never written.

Though the *Chronicle* editors rejected the demands, they made several gestures to show respect towards those who had assailed them and to express concern for their feelings. Despite the threatened boycott, the *Chronicle* was not hostile in its response. "We're sorry that our friends and peers are hurt by this advertisement," *Chronicle* editor Greg Pessin said. "Many people are offended by many things the *Chronicle* runs each day. . . . [But] open debate should not be sacrificed for comfort. Although many members of our community were deeply offended by the ad, that does not mean that Mr. Horowitz's views, no matter how offensive, should not have been aired."[126] Pessin and three other senior-level editors later hand-delivered a statement to Black Student Alliance president Denis Antoine, which repeated the apology: "We're sorry members of our community were offended and hurt by this advertisement."[127]

Reading the account of the black students' vigil, I have as much feeling for these youngsters driven to tears by my words as anyone in my shoes could. But my feelings are infused with ambivalence and overlaid with questions. "Being black is a huge part of my identity," protest leader Sarah Wigfall told a *Chronicle* reporter. "I was utterly offended and disgusted by what was put in the paper."[128] But why? Tears might be understandable as a response, say, to "slavery denial." Tears might be an understandable response to a justification of slavery. But why in the world should pointing out the obvious—that slavery is long since over, and that post-slavery America has brought bounties to blacks—why should *this* cause people to cry? Is it because they fear that the umbilical link to victimhood

124. *Chronicle*, 23 March 2001.
125. Ibid.
126. *Chronicle*, 22 March 2001.
127. *Chronicle*, 23 March 2001.
128. Ibid.

will be cut and they will be forced into the moral complexity of full citizenship—a status their mentors have purposefully withheld from them?

The fact is that far from being members of a helpless victim class at Duke, Sarah Wigfall and her fellow protesters are privileged youth, attending an elite university where the cost of an education is over $100,000. The beneficiaries of years of efforts by whites as well as blacks, many are on full scholarships provided by the school *because* they are minorities. In the Duke environment, these students are hardly afflicted by racial oppression. The overture made by the editors who printed the ad and the response of the Duke administration show enormous concern for individuals making outrageous demands—insisting on the suppression of ideas in a university setting and the creation of segregated facilities (while at the same time complaining about not feeling "welcome").

While a student activist in the 1960s, I do not remember receiving private communiqués from university presidents to salve my hurt feelings when my radical demands weren't met. I do not remember these officials offering university funds to help us publish our protests. Back then, we radicals were tolerated for what we were—people whose objectives were at odds with free intellectual inquiry and inimical to the uses of the university. Today, the opposite is true. Student radicals blackmail administrators at will and administrators create the intellectual atmosphere that invites such blackmail. In contrast to the exaggerated concern shown for these students' sensibilities—a sort of entitlement in today's university—I did not receive a single communication during the entire controversy from university officials apologizing for the damage their institutions inflicted on my reputation or the threats their campuses presented to my safety. Nor did a single college editor apologize for the smears published in their papers. Nor was I invited to speak at a single one of the university forums that schools like Duke sponsored to discuss my ad.

I certainly didn't like the idea of young people standing around in tears, but the question remains: What were they crying *about?*

Part of the explanation could be found in their instruction from the university about "words that wound" (and its subtext that there is power in being wounded). *Words That Wound* is the title of a seminal book written by four radical law professors whose views inspired the adoption of "speech codes" in hundreds of universities across the country during the 1980s.[129] They argued that some words in some contexts are actually not

---

129. M. J. Matsuda, C. R. Lawrence III, R. Delgado and K. W. Crenshaw, *Words That Wound: Critical Race Theory, Assaultive Speech and the First Amendment* (Boulder, 1993). Cf. the discussion of these doctrines in Martin P. Golding, *Free Speech on Campus* (New York, 2000).

just words at all, but a form of harassment, and thus a form of racial and sexual "oppression" for which redress is required. This notion eventually led to the creation of an extensive apparatus of review and punishment throughout the university system. Though it did not include words or sentiments that came under the codes, my ad was an expression of "politically incorrect" views that the students thought should come under similar ban.

The pseudo-judicial courts and restrictive speech codes that were implemented in universities in the 1980s eventually came under legal attack by a countermovement.[130] In fact, the Individual Rights Foundation, an organization I created, played a significant role in ridding California institutions of their own speech codes. In 1993, as part of a suit settlement, our lawyers forced a vice chancellor at the University of California's Riverside campus to undergo five hours of "sensitivity training in the First Amendment" because he had punished a fraternity for designing a T-shirt campus leftists didn't like. The embarrassment that university officials suffered at the hands of an amused press corps warned others against making the same mistake.[131] Campus speech codes have been in retreat ever since, but the victories over them remain illusory, since their residue lives on not only in the structures that remain, but in attitudes more oppressive and more effective in embargoing ideas than those of the McCarthy era.[132]

Another troubling source of the hypersensitivity around racial issues is the university curriculum itself. In virtually every discipline of social study the dominant academic doctrines conform to the categories of a racial Marxism in which a dominant (white) race and a dominant (male) gender rule as masters over every other. These disciplines include "whiteness studies," "critical race studies," "postcolonial studies," "women's studies" and various "postmodernist" perspectives. Through prisms like these the American past and present can look very grim to undergraduates innocent of the historical record. "The political history of the United States [proclaims a feminist law professor at Georgetown Law, a Jesuit institution and one of the most prestigious law schools in the country] is in large measure a history of almost unthinkable brutality towards slaves, genocidal hatred of Native Americans, racist devaluation of nonwhites

130. Harvey Silverglate and Alan Kors, *The Shadow University* (New York, 1998). Daphne Patai, *Heterophobia* (New York, 1998).
131. Ralph Frammolino, "Free Speech Suit Ends Ban on UC Riverside Fraternity," *Los Angeles Times*, 11 November 1993.
132. Silverglate and Kors, *The Shadow University*.

and nonwhite cultures [and] sexist devaluation of women. . . . [American history] is a history of ruthlessness; of brutality; and of mindless, infantile, and at times psychotic, numbing wrath."[133] Rarely has there been a more succinct summary of the "progressive" worldview.

■   ■

In the midst of the controversy at Duke, the powerful influence of these hostile themes was dramatized by the publication of the first professorial rebuttal to my ad. It appeared as a letter to the editor in the March 29 issue of the *Duke Chronicle*. The author was John Hope Franklin, the James B. Duke Professor of History Emeritus, and one of the university's most celebrated academic figures. Professor Franklin was the author of a classic text, *From Slavery to Freedom*, and the most honored African-American historian of slavery alive. He was the only living faculty member at Duke to have an academic center named after him. One of the ironies of the events surrounding the placement of my ad was that the Duke administration responded to the protests against it by increasing the university's financial support for the John Hope Franklin Center for Interdisciplinary and International Studies.[134]

Franklin was also the former head of President Clinton's "Commission on Race and Reconciliation," which was tasked with carrying on a "national dialogue on race," but only achieved a monologue because Franklin refused to include Ward Connerly and other critics of his own perspective. His 500-word statement condemning my ad was circulated via the Internet to Afro-American Studies departments at other colleges, and its ideas appeared in published and posted responses to my ad on campuses across the country.

Horowitz's Diatribe Contains Historical Inaccuracies[135]

By John Hope Franklin

Here are a few things to bear in mind when reading the diatribe on slavery and reparations that appeared in the *Chronicle* a few days ago.

All whites and no slaves benefited from American slavery. All blacks had no rights that they could claim as their own. All whites, including

---

133. Robin West, *Progressive Constitutionalism: Reconstructing the Fourteenth Amendment* (Durham, N.C., 1994), pp. 17–18.
134. "Keohane Issues Report on Racial Issues at Duke."
135. Franklin's letter was prominently posted on the official website of the John Hope Franklin Center of International and Inter-Disciplinary studies at Duke. www.duke.edu/web/jhfcenter/main.html.

the vast majority who had no slaves, were not only encouraged but authorized to exercise dominion over all slaves, thereby adding strength to the system of control.

If David Horowitz had read James D. DeBow's *The Interest in Slavery of the Southern Non-slaveholder*, he would not have blundered into the fantasy of claiming that no single group benefited from slavery. Planters did, of course. New York merchants did, of course. Even poor whites benefited from the legal advantage they enjoyed over all blacks as well as from the psychological advantage of having a group beneath them. Meanwhile, laws enacted by states forbade the teaching of blacks any means of acquiring knowledge—including the alphabet—which is the legacy of disadvantage of educational privatization and discrimination experienced by African-Americans in 2001.

Most living Americans do have a connection with slavery. They have inherited the preferential advantage, if they are white, or the loathsome disadvantage, if they are black; and those positions are virtually as alive today as they were in the 19th century. The pattern of housing, the discrimination in employment, the resistance to equal opportunity in education, the racial profiling, the inequities in the administration of justice, the low expectation of blacks in the discharge of duties assigned to them, the widespread belief that blacks have physical prowess but little intellectual capacities and the widespread opposition to affirmative action, as if that had not been enjoyed by whites for three centuries, all indicate that the vestiges of slavery are still with us.

And as long as there are pro-slavery protagonists among us, hiding behind such absurdities as "we are all in this together" or "it hurts me as much as it hurts you" or "slavery benefited you as much as it benefited me," we will suffer from the inability to confront the tragic legacies of slavery and deal with them in a forthright and constructive manner.

Most important, we must never fall victim to some scheme designed to create a controversy among potential allies in order to divide them and, at the same time, exploit them for its own special purpose.

John Hope Franklin
James B. Duke Professor Emeritus
John Hope Franklin Center for Interdisciplinary
and International Studies

Franklin's opening statement in this appalling document—that "all whites and no slaves benefited from American slavery"—sidestepped the argument and was, in any case, irrelevant to the dispute itself. No one would argue that slaves benefited from their own slavery. Franklin's statement that "*all* whites" had benefited, on the other hand, was the claim of a racial ideologue rather than a responsible historian who would want to keep an open mind on the question of whether all whites had in fact benefited from slavery (or, for that matter, whether any free blacks had). Did a dirt-poor squatter in the Dakota territory circa 1860 really get some kind of psychological boost from the fact that blacks were enslaved two thousand miles away?

In any case, Franklin failed to answer the question I had posed in my ad: If all whites alive today are beneficiaries of the wealth that slavery produced, how can one maintain that blacks alive today are not as well? How was the wealth passed through white hands only? How did a black worker in a tobacco state not benefit from the investment that slavers had made?

Franklin's assertion that "all blacks had no rights that they could claim as their own" is simply false. Even the African slaves from the slave ship *Amistad*, who were not U.S. citizens, had rights that were recognized by the Supreme Court, which (with a slaveholding majority presiding) voted to free them. Hundreds of thousands of free blacks in America had citizen rights, including the right to own slaves, as more than three thousand did.[136] Though free blacks could not vote in many states, some, like Frederick Douglass, were respected statesmen in their own right. Even chattel slaves in the Deep South had rights as human beings that the law bound their masters to respect. As a historian of slavery living in North Carolina should know, the American Revolution changed British law *specifically* to recognize the humanity and rights of African slaves:

> In North Carolina, in 1774, the punishment for killing a slave "willfully and maliciously" was a year's imprisonment; and the murderer was required to pay the owner the value of the slave. In 1791, the state's legislature denounced this law as "disgraceful to humanity and degrading in the highest degree to the laws and principles of a free,

---

136. It is argued endlessly on the other side of this dispute (see Chrisman and Allen, for example) that black slaveholding was benevolent because blacks bought family members to free them. There is truth in this claim, but only a partial one. The most authoritative study of black slaveowners in South Carolina has this to say: "The census of 1850 demonstrated that 83.1 percent of the Negro masters were mulattoes, while nearly 90 percent of their slaves were of dark skin. Where was the kinship? Since mulattoes primarily married mulattoes, the black fold owned by light-skinned Afro-Americans were seldom kin and were overwhelmingly held as laborers. By and large, Negro slaveowners were darker copies of their white counterparts." Larry Koger, *Black Slaveowners: Free Black Slave Masters in South Carolina, 1790–1860* (Columbia, S.C., 1985).

Christian, and enlightened country" because it drew a "distinction of criminality between the murder of a white person and of one who is *equally an human creature, but merely of a different complexion.*" Thereupon, by law, it was murder to kill a slave willfully and maliciously.[137] [emphasis added]

Another meaningless claim in Franklin's argument is the statement that "all whites, including the vast majority who had no slaves, were not only encouraged but authorized to exercise dominion over all slaves, thereby adding strength to the system of control." But whites who were so encouraged often took the opposite course: resistance to, subversion of, and finally war against slavery, and did so in enough numbers to put an end to the system. Hundreds of thousands of whites died in these struggles. It is the denial of this reality that is the heart of the dispute.

Franklin's list of whites who benefited from slavery is also irrelevant, since the statement in the ad was not that no whites benefited from slavery, but—to repeat—that free blacks and the free descendants of black slaves did. As noted earlier, Franklin does not even address this argument.

Franklin's claim that "most living Americans do have a connection with slavery" is really two claims: that slavery and racism are identical—which is a problematic thesis—and that racism in American society has remained virtually unchanged since the nineteenth century, which is false.

There is something almost pathological in Franklin's remark that all blacks inherit "the loathsome disadvantage" of being black. Franklin, who is black, has been honored all his professional life, and beyond all his white professional colleagues at Duke. He is the most celebrated figure in a southern institution named after James B. Duke (the benefactor of his own professorship) whose fortune was built on tobacco wealth, one of the chief crops of the very system that brought Franklin's ancestors to this continent in chains. John Hope Franklin's inability to appreciate these ironies (or to applaud his own good fortune) reveals a disconcerting failure of historical rectitude and imagination.

Franklin's final claim is a ludicrous insinuation that I (and by extension anyone who disagrees with his views on reparations) am a "proslavery antagonist." When stripped of its intellectual pretension, this argument is no different from the gutter talk of any racial demagogue.

---

137. Lawrence M. Friedman, *Crime and Punishment in American History* (New York, 1993), pp. 90–91. Cited in Thomas G. West, *Vindicating the Founders* (New York, 1997), p. 13.

The most pernicious aspect of this bitter and graceless screed, however, is reserved for its closing flourish. Franklin advises black students to avoid "controversy" among themselves, stamp out the diversity of viewpoints, and essentially embrace a totalitarian unity. It is the sort of attitude that leads to charges of "race treason" against those who fail to uphold the groupthink. In his other life on the president's race panel, it allowed Franklin to treat an independent mind like Ward Connerly as having "nothing to contribute."[138] Such a statement summarized the outlook that attacked the ad and the editors who gave it a hearing.

138. Ward Connerly, *Creating Equal: My Fight Against Race Preferences* (San Francisco, 2000), p. 5

*I am not tragically colored. There is no great sorrow dammed up
in my soul, nor lurking behind my eyes.... I do not belong to the
sobbing school of Negro-hood who hold that nature somehow
has given them a low-down dirty deal and whose feelings are all
hurt about. Even in the helter-skelter skirmish that is my life, I
have seen that the world is to the strong regardless of a little
pigmentation more or less. No, I do not weep at the world—I
am too busy sharpening my oyster knife.*
Zora Neale Hurston, "How It Feels to Be Colored Me"

SIX

RACISM AND FREE SPEECH

I had been criticized for writing an ad that was "insensitive" to blacks, and yet I had been motivated to write the ad, in part, because I felt the reparations argument was calculated to separate blacks from other Americans, from their American heritage and from their place in the "American dream." I decided to fashion another ad out of these points that would emphasize this (positive) side of the argument. I called it "The Debt" and submitted it to eight new schools, including the *Daily Tar Heel* at the University of North Carolina.[139]

The Debt[140]
Some African-American leaders are calling for reparations to be paid to American blacks by the U.S. government and therefore by other Americans—of European, Asian, Hispanic and Native American descent. Slavery was a crime against humanity, but it was ended by

---

139. The others were the *American Eagle* at American University, which printed it, and the *Columbia Spectator*, the *Berkeley Daily Californian*, the *Wisconsin Daily Cardinal*, the *Virginia Cavalier*, the *Washington Daily* and the *Cornell Sun*, which did not. Harvard, which had rejected the original ad, printed this one as an op-ed column.
140. I have rearranged a sentence or two for readability and have excised two paragraphs which refer to Randall Robinson's attack on Thomas Jefferson, an issue that is dealt with below.

this same government over 136 years ago. There are no slaves or children of slaves alive today to receive such reparations.

On the other hand, blacks now living in America are the freest and most prosperous black people on earth. The average descendant of African slaves in America earns between 20 and 50 times as much as the average black person in Africa, whose ancestors were not kidnapped and enslaved.... For African-Americans to pursue "reparations" claims against European, Asian, and Hispanic Americans is a divisive and self-defeating idea. Why do African-American leaders want to separate African-Americans from other Americans? Blacks came before the Mayflower. Who is more American than the descendants of African slaves?

Behind the reparations [movement], finally, is an irrational fear and hatred of America. It is about holding America responsible for every negative facet of black existence, as though America were God, and God had failed. Above all, it is about denying the gift America has given to all of its citizens, black as well as white, through the inspired genius of its founding.... For all America's faults, African-Americans have an enormous stake in America and in [its] heritage....

The heritage enshrined in the American founding and the institutions and ideas to which it gave rise is what is really under attack in the reparations movement. This assault on America, led by racial separatists and the political left, is not only an attack on white Americans, but on all Americans—and on African-Americans especially. America's black citizens are the richest and most privileged black people alive—a bounty that is a direct result of the heritage that is under assault. The American idea needs the support of its African-American citizens. But African-Americans also need the support of the American idea.

If anyone thought that changing the somewhat astringent tone of the original ad would have changed the response, however, the reception of this version suggested otherwise. Under the spell of campus Marxism many students protesting the original text had also objected to the fact that it *was* an ad—and that I had paid for it. Even if the text itself had not been "offensive," the monetary transaction would have presented a problem. "You say you want to encourage open debate, but it's not a debate when someone spends $1,000," complained student leader Patricia Chen at one of the Duke demonstrations.[141] By taking out an ad, these

---

141. *Duke Chronicle*, 22 March 2001. Chen was president of the Asian American Students Association at Duke.

opponents argued, I had "bought speech." An ad, they suggested counterintuitively, conveyed more authority than a column, and was therefore doubly unfair. While events at Duke were unfolding, the editors of the *Daily Tar Heel* at the University of North Carolina tested all these propositions.

Tar Heel editor Matt Dees was particularly determined to thread the needle where editors on other papers had failed. He thought the new version was "[not] nearly as inflammatory as the [original] ad" but, even so, refused the money I offered. He then ran "The Debt" as an op-ed column. To make sure that its publication did not seem like an editorial endorsement, he also invited two student leaders, Tyra Moore and Doug Taylor,[142] to write a much longer critique of what I had written, to be printed alongside it.

To make even more certain that he was in the clear, Dees ran a statement by UNC chancellor James Moeser in the same issue of the *Tar Heel*. The statement dropped the mask of administration neutrality and characterized my views as "despicable and shameful, diminishing the cost of slavery and damaging the self-respect of an entire race."[143] Of course the chancellor was also interested in covering himself. After delivering this slap in the face, he defended my free speech.

But if Dees thought the campus radicals would let him off the hook, he had another think coming. "The *Daily Tar Heel*, and editor Matt Dees in particular, has been duped," declared a columnist in the same issue in fractured English. "An ignorant, egotistical bully has conned the *Daily Tar Heel* into furthering his views. And the *Daily Tar Heel* didn't even take his money."[144] Even more ungratefully, Tyra Moore and Doug Taylor, the student leaders he had invited into his pages to disinfect it of my ideas, attacked Dees and the *Tar Heel* as "racist." Their column (printed in the same issue) was imaginatively titled: "Students Must Unite to Fight Hate."[145] It was little wonder that Dees felt stabbed in the back, as he explained:

> Before delving into an explanation of our decision to run David Horowitz's views, I must say that I feel slightly betrayed by Tyra Moore and company. I thought that by giving them the opportunity to refute

---

142. Their movement was called "On the Wake of Emancipation."

143. James Moeser, "UNC Should Foster Intellectual Debate," *Daily Tar Heel*, 2 April 2001.

144. Brian Frederick, "Running Horowitz Column Gave Legitimacy to His Views," *Daily Tar Heel*, 18 April 2001. Frederick was the "Reader's Advocate" for the *Tar Heel* and a journalism student.

145. *Daily Tar Heel*, 2 April 2001.

Horowitz's claims the day they ran, a privilege given by no other college newspaper—to my knowledge—they would respect our decision to run his views in the name of free speech and open discussion.... But you know what they say about assumptions. Moore and friends apparently could not resist attacking this paper as racist, a charge that is unfair, unfounded and downright infuriating. Shame on them.[146]

By bending over backwards to his radical tormentors, Dees had hoped to avoid the demonstrations that rocked Duke and other campuses. But he was to be disappointed in this expectation as well. On the day the columns appeared, more than a hundred students, mostly black, marched around campus with a *non sequitur* chant, "Education is a right, not just for the rich and white!"[147] It was an omnibus protest against the ad and for better wages for the housekeepers and groundskeepers employed by UNC. ("The university was built by slaves in 1793," Tyra Moore and Doug Taylor had digressed in their column. "Over 200 years later the descendants of those slaves, the housekeepers and groundskeepers, still struggle to make a living wage here at the University.")

But the final word on the antics at UNC, as far as I was concerned, came from a Chapel Hill resident who was not part of the university community:

> I am a 45-year-old black man. I want to commend the *Daily Tar Heel* for running the David Horowitz column. I have followed Horowitz's writing before he ever got involved with the reparations issue. I have studied closely his remarks on reparations, not only his ad but subsequent remarks on television and on college campuses. His remarks are not racist.
>
> As a black man, I have experienced racism—so I know what it is. I do not hesitate to confront it (provided it's not more profitable to sidestep it) when I meet it. But there is something far worse than racism going on. That is the cravenly, knee-jerk reaction of college students to issues they don't like....
>
> If Horowitz is wrong, it should not take a great deal of effort to expose him.... Students are in college to learn, and this could be a great learning experience on how to dismantle a defective argument, if indeed it is defective.... But we do not seem to have real students.

146. Matt Dees, "Disagree, Debate, But Don't Kill the Messenger," *Daily Tar Heel,* 2 April 2001.
147. "UNC-CH Protest Seeks Better Climate for Blacks," *Raleigh News & Observer,* 3 April 2001.

We do not seem to have people who want to learn. What we do seem to have is a bunch of conformist, rigid, unimaginative drones who want to make others do what they want or stop them from being heard. This generation scares me. They are too weak-minded to deal with reality. . . .

Black people of years past put in a lot of pain, blood, sweat and tears to attain what we have now. It's not perfect, but it is certainly better. Is this all we have to show for it, a generation of spoiled, easily offended brats who'd rather coerce than think? . . .

Bruce Newman[148]

■   ■

Two days after Matt Dees' effort to appease the left failed, Daniel Stephens and the editors of the *Daily Princetonian* tried yet another tack. Unlike Dees, Stephens and the Princeton editors were leftists, which put them in the same bind as UC Berkeley's Daniel Hernandez. As aspiring journalists, they did not want to appear too disrespectful of the freedoms of the Fourth Estate. Nor did they want to stray too far from the party line of political correctness. The *Princetonians* took a middle—and hypocritical—path, claiming that I had tied their hands and forced them to print the ad against their will:

> Horowitz plays a clever game. He played it with several of our peer college papers in the past few weeks. And he won. When Horowitz submits an ad to a college paper, he hopes that one of two things will happen: Either the paper refuses to print the ad, so he can tell the world that conservative ideas are being censored by the liberal college press, or the paper prints the ad and campus activists protest. Both ways, Horowitz gets what he wants: his name in the news and his message in the national media. . . . In no way do we support Horowitz's argument. Denying publication of the ad, however, just gives Horowitz what he is looking for: another reason to cry "censor."[149]

The *Princetonian* solution to the dilemma was to publish the ad while preemptively defaming me as a "racist." To emphasize the point, they decided to take my tainted money, but turn it over—as reparations—to an appropriately symbolic group:

---

148. *Daily Tar Heel,* 6 April 2001.
149. "A Message to Our Readers," *Daily Princetonian,* 4 April 2001.

In a gesture that we hope will demonstrate to our readers our com-
mitment to open dialogue, but also our own integrity as a campus
publication, we have decided not to keep the money that Horowitz's
group paid for the ad. Instead, we donate the proceeds from the ad
to the Trenton chapter of the National Urban League, a non-profit,
non-partisan group that works for civil rights and racial understanding. We do not want to profit from Horowitz's racism. Donating the
money seems like the right thing to do.

When I read the editorial, I told my office to put a stop-payment on
the check. If I was going to make a donation it would be to the inner-city
organizations working with disadvantaged black and Hispanic youngsters
in Los Angeles with whom I had been associated for years. I had no intention of giving money to the Urban League, which had just launched a campaign against the standardized college entrance tests called SATs. These
tests historically had been designed to help minorities who faced discrimination gain entrance to elite institutions like Princeton, which had excluded
blacks, Jews and other "undesirables" in the past. By substituting objec-
tive, merit-based tests for subjective assessments, reformers had successfully overcome these barriers. The present attack on the SATs had been
prompted by the poor test scores of black high school students, which
kept them from entering better colleges. But eliminating the SATs would
do nothing to fix the problem, which stemmed from poor public schools
and weak family support. Lowering the bar—as author John McWhorter
has observed—never encouraged anyone to achieve more.[150] Far from
helping black youth, the Urban League's campaign would hurt them.

Some conservatives criticized my decision not to pay for the ad. True
to their principles, the Republican students at Brown, for example, complained that I had violated the "sanctity of contract." In my view, it was
more a case of damaged goods. I was particularly irked that the *Princetonian*'s response to the ad did not contain a single reference to what I
had said. I may have upset conservatives' sense of propriety and of property rights, but I was not going to pay for abuse.

Whatever the reasons—guilt? embarrassment?—the *Princetonian*
agreed one week later to print a piece of mine as submitted. In it, I addressed
an issue that had surfaced regularly in the exchanges over my ad. This was
the question as to whether I, as a Jew, was opposed to Holocaust reparations for Jews. There is an ugly current of anti-Semitism in the literature

---

150. Remarks to the Wednesday Morning Club, Los Angeles, 17 May 2001. See also John
McWhorter, *Losing the Race* (New York, 2000).

of black separatism which seemed to surface in the reparations movement. It took the form of an obsessive harping on Jews having received payments that blacks were denied. At one point in my MIT debate, for instance, Dorothy Benton-Lewis (head of the National Coalition of Blacks for Reparations in America) had said:

> No, we did not benefit from slavery. No more than the Jewish people benefited from the European Holocaust, nor the Native Americans from their near extermination, nor the Russian [Jews] from anti-Semitism, the Russian [Jews] that we airlifted and reestablished in the millions in Israel. Yes, it has been awhile, but 135 years is a different yardstick for Africans. And we spend billions of dollars, year after year, to reestablish a state called Israel, based on a 2,000-year-old Biblical reference. 135 [vs.] 2000. I think that's a different yardstick, and we're not gonna have it. Reparations are due."[151]

My answer was that Jews who had received reparations for the Holocaust were direct survivors, "individuals who had their property and lives taken from them." The state of Israel had received reparations because it was "a state built by survivors of the Holocaust, and because no other state would provide refuge for Jews during the Holocaust." Neither I nor any other Jews had received reparations merely for being Jews. Nor would I accept reparations if they were offered. "I would not only refuse to accept them," I wrote, "but I would take out an ad calling it a bad idea for Jews and racist too."

I also used the column to talk about the debt that even those minorities who suffered injustice in America owed to this country:

> As a Jew, I know that whatever injustices my people have suffered in this country, America is the best, freest and safest place for Jews to live in the entire world. As a Jew I owe a debt to America for giving me the opportunities and freedoms I have and for creating a society that is a paragon of tolerance compared to any other place I know. It is my opinion that black Americans—who are richer, freer and safer in America than they would be anywhere else on earth—should feel the same way.[152]

I urged the members of the Princeton community "to support not only my right to express these views, but to express them without being

151. MIT debate, http://video.C-span.org:8080/ramgen/ndrive/e040701_slavery.rm.
152. "Horowitz Responds to Princetonian's 'Abuse,'" *Daily Princetonian*, 9 April 2001.

subjected to character assassination and abuse." This was the only way "to protect the free speech rights of every member of this community." But the *Princetonian* editors did not experience any change of heart. Two weeks later, I had the opportunity to bait the tiger in its lair when I was invited by a group of Princeton conservatives who called themselves the "Whigs and Clios" to debate Dorothy Benton-Lewis again. In a typical display of cowardice, the *Princetonian* editors organized a forum to discuss my ad, and convened it directly after my event, but did not invite me to participate.[153]

In my opening remarks, I scolded the *Princetonian* editors for the hate speech in their editorial against me. I drew attention to the fact that philosophy professor Robert George was the only open conservative on the Princeton faculty. This was a disgrace, and it diminished their education. This fact provided an instructive background to the current controversy. I criticized the faculty for its absolute silence while principles it pretended to hold sacred were under attack. I singled out one professor in particular, Sean Wilentz, who had made a spectacle of himself during the impeachment proceedings by posturing as a champion of democracy and warning Republican congressmen that history would "hunt you down" for failing to defend the principles of the republic. Where was he in *this* battle for free speech, taking place in his own institution?

My debating partner, Dorothy Benton-Lewis, was as courteous in our exchange as she had been before, while her views remained as extreme as ever. At one point she argued that Americans should return the land to the Indians and "pay rent" to them.

There were no student protests at Princeton. Daniel Stephens and his co-editors had stumbled onto a solution to the problem I had "forced" on them. To satisfy the left—and prevent demonstrations—they parroted the party line and did the name-calling themselves.

■   ■

The attacks on the reparations ad were more extensive and had attracted more attention than any previous campus incident involving freedom of the press or free speech. Yet they were not a new or isolated phenomenon. According to the Student Press Law Center, an organization that provides free legal help to student papers under attack, there have been 205 incidents

---

153. At Arizona State and UC Santa Barbara, leftist professors held panels and "teach-ins" on the ad during the time I spoke, in a futile effort to draw the crowds away. At Arizona State, the left flew radical professor Michael Eric Dyson from St. Paul to attack me a week after I was there.

of "offensive" student papers being stolen and burned since 1993.[154] In one celebrated case, black students destroyed 14,000 copies of the *Daily Pennsylvanian* because they were upset over the appearance of two op-ed columns by the same author. One had criticized Martin Luther King's personal ethics; the other had challenged the racial double standards displayed by the University of Pennsylvania authorities when they failed to discipline a black honor society called Onyx whose members had hazed blindfolded initiates and shouted anti-white slogans in the middle of the night, waking up students in the dorms. No actions were brought against the members of Onyx, but the author of the columns was investigated for thirty-four student-initiated charges of "racial harassment" for what he had written. (The charges were eventually dismissed.)[155]

While racial issues were obviously a factor prompting the efforts to suppress my ad, these efforts would have been made even if race had been no part of the issue at all. That someone should challenge the hegemony of the left on campus was enough to invite retribution. This was made clear by a new ad campaign conducted by members of the Independent Women's Forum during the last weeks of the spring semester. The IWF attempted to place an ad titled "Take Back the Campus! Combat the Radical Feminist Assault on the Truth" in five college papers. The ad was written by Christina Hoff Sommers, author of two well-known books that had angered radical feminists, *Who Stole Feminism?* and *The War Against Boys*. Taking a cue from my efforts, the IWF ad listed the "Ten Most Common Feminist Myths," among them the claim that one in four women was a rape victim and that women earned only 75 percent of what men were paid. (In fact, if work experience, skill level, and educational background were taken into account, women earned about 98 percent what men did, according to government figures.) The *Columbia Spectator* rejected the IWF ad; the *Harvard Crimson* wanted changes made that were not approved by the time the school year ended; the *Dartmouth Review,* the *Yale Daily News* and the *UCLA Daily Bruin* all published it.[156]

The response at UCLA was particularly revealing. A demonstration was held to protest what the organizers described as "hateful misinformation," "hostile" and "violent."[157] They demanded a free page to respond

---

154. Nat Hentoff, "Ruffian Fake Radicals," *Village Voice,* 24 April 2001.
155. Silverglate and Kors, *The Shadow University,* pp. 20–21.
156. www.IWF.org. Mason Stockstill, "Students Protest Publication of Ad in Newspaper," *Daily Bruin Online,* 21 May 2001.
157. Scott B. Wong, "Women's Groups Demand Apology from Bruin for Ad," *Daily Bruin Online,* 17 May 2001.

and—citing the precedent set by Daniel Hernandez—an apology from the paper's editors as well. One of the student leaders, Christie Scott, told a reporter the IWF statement was "just as detrimental as the Horowitz ad" and reiterated: "We ... want an apology, but most of all we want this not to happen again."[158] The most ominous statement came from LeAnn Quinn, a psychology senior and member of the Coalition for the Fair Representation of Women, who said: "They're trying to infiltrate campuses with their lies and myths."[159] Defense of the university as a fortress of left-wing purity indicated how far doctrines of political correctness had themselves "infiltrated" the education of undergraduates at UCLA.

It also showed that the underlying issue in the controversies over the ad was ultimately not racial, but political. Civil libertarian Nat Hentoff drew attention to this fact in noting the ironic parallel between the attacks on the campus papers that printed the reparations ad and the destruction of abolitionist newspapers by pro-slavery mobs in the era before the Civil War.[160] Writing in the New York *Village Voice,* Hentoff described a meeting he had attended at Columbia University, hosted by the International Socialist Organization, a campus player in the events at Brown and the attacks on student papers at other colleges.[161] The ISO flier advertising the event proclaimed: "Right-Wingers Try to Buy Free Speech! Anti-Racist Protester from Brown Speaks Out!"

Buying space for a political ad was actually not that different from submitting an article, except that it allowed the purchaser to publish his opinions more swiftly and efficiently, and it allowed editors to establish some distance from the contents. This relieved the editors of some of their oversight responsibilities while allowing the writer more freedom in expressing his views. On the other hand, both the op-ed column and the ad purchase were privileges, not rights. Every paper has the right to reject any ad it chooses and any article as well. The First Amendment enjoins government from interfering with free speech. It does not compel editors to publish everything submitted to them. There is one caveat, however, because

---

158. *Daily Bruin Online,* 17 May 2001.
159. Ibid.
160. Hentoff, "Ruffian Fake Radicals"; cf. Michael Kent Curtis, *Free Speech* (University of Kentucky, 2001).
161. The *Columbia Spectator* had rejected the reparations ad. Like many such papers, however, it had assigned its reporters to cover the story of the controversy, while ready access to the Internet allowed anyone interested on campus to see the ad itself. The *Spectator's* refusal to run the ad was ostensibly based on a policy of not printing any political ads and after some negotiation it finally did agree to open the pages of its summer edition to an op-ed column I wrote on the controversy.

the courts have held that if a paper is funded and overseen by a state institution and prints an ad on one side of a political debate, it cannot deny
ad space to the other side. I was able to use this ruling in the case of the
Minnesota Daily at the University of Minnesota. The *Daily* originally
rejected the ad, but after being apprised of the law, agreed to print it.[162]

The issue of free speech arose in the case of my ad, not because I had
a right to have it printed, but because there was a concerted political effort
to prevent me from doing so. At the Columbia protest event, the Brown
activist said: "The *Village Voice* printed the ad, and we need to organize
against it and shut the paper down!"[163] Commented Hentoff: "This is
hardly the first time that there have been threats to shut us down, but the
totalitarian mind-set of these traducers of the civil rights movement on
campuses around the country is worth more attention than has been paid
by the mainstream press."

The failure to confront the "totalitarian" dimension of the controversy made the press treatment somewhat less reassuring than would otherwise have been the case. It was one thing to provide a vigorous defense
of anyone's right to say anything (he may be a "racist" but let him speak).
It was quite another to defend the integrity of views that were under attack.
Suppose radicals hadn't stolen the paper at Brown, or demonstrated at the
editorial offices of the *Duke Chronicle,* and suppose the editor of the *Daily
Californian* had not apologized under pressure. Few people would have
heard about the ad. But more importantly, fewer still would be aware that
forty campus papers had refused to run a perfectly reasonable statement
for fear of being labeled "racist" by unscrupulous censors.

Among all the editorial defenses of the ad in *USA Today,* the *Boston
Globe,* the *Philadelphia Inquirer* and other papers, none found anything
racist in the ad itself. Yet none defended the ad (or its author) against the
racial smears either. In other words, no one defended my right to make a
reasonable argument on an issue like reparations without being subject to
racial attacks. In my view, this was almost as important as the right to
publish the ad itself.

The problem was underscored by a backhanded defense of my speech
rights in a *Newsweek* column by Jonathan Alter.[164] In the center of the
page on which the column appeared there was a photograph of one of the

162. This aspect of the controversy was covered by the Internet journal *DiversityInc.com.*
Candice Choi, "Anti-Reparations Ads Protected under First Amendment, Author
Argues," 6 April 2001.
163. In fact, the ad was never submitted to the *Voice.*
164. Jonathan Alter, "Where PC Meets Free Speech," *Newsweek,* 2 April 2001.

Spartacist protesters at Berkeley. She was carrying a sign that said in big letters: "David Horowitz, Racist Ideologue." There was no caption to the photograph, and there was no reference to the photo in Alter's piece. In other words, none of the four million readers of *Newsweek* was informed that this woman belonged to a totalitarian sect, was a self-described "communist" who wanted a Bolshevik America, and was prepared to denounce anyone whose views opposed her own as a "tool of the bosses" and a "racist."

On the other hand, the same media that subliminally spread these slanders would not have dared to characterize the minority students and faculty who smeared me as hate-mongers.[165] That would fall under the category of "insensitive." Yet I was the one in danger of being marginalized as a "bigot."

This was not a concern easily dismissed. My career as a writer and commentator is dependent in part on the attitudes of thousands of people in media and political circles who know me only by reputation. In innumerable incidents like the *Newsweek* photo, the reputation I depended on was being injured in ways I had no means to redress. How many editors, after seeing Alter's article, would think a second time before asking me to write? What institutions would decide not to invite me to speak because of my "controversial" image? Which politicians would avoid me in order to forestall the possibility of guilt by association? I would never know.

The column that Alter had written was itself an exercise in McCarthyism, racial and otherwise. He began by misrepresenting me as an "agitator" of the "extreme right." In fact I have a middle-of-the-road position on abortion, libertarian views on issues of media censorship, and a long record of defending gays against right-wing attacks. I am also an outspoken critic of Republicans for not being concerned enough about the plight of minorities in America's inner cities.[166] This last fact is material because of the concluding paragraph in Alter's column which attributed to me a view that was the opposite of everything I had ever said or believed: "The not-so-subtle subtext [of the ad] was that we've given 'them' enough, and so should give up on addressing the continuing problems of race and poverty in America." To drive home this idea, without any supporting

---

165. The woman carrying the sign, along with most of the Spartacists, was white.

166. I have written about the plight of inner-city schools and urged Republicans to take up this cause in particular in *The Art of Political War* (Dallas, 2000), pp. 52 et seq. In my plan to "reshape the Republican Party" in the same volume, point 2 of a recommended Republican agenda is: "Give minorities and the poor a shot at the American Dream." (p. 35)

evidence, Alter wrote: "The ad reminds me of one of those tiresome rants supporting a NAAWP (National Association for the Advancement of White People)."

Alter could easily have consulted the hundreds of thousands of words I had written on the Internet, which refuted his claim. But even this "research" was unnecessary since my ad itself provided a rebuttal. Its text was difficult, in fact, to misread. Its final point emphasized that there was no group with a longer-standing claim to be American than African-Americans. I had said that America needed African-Americans as much as African-Americans needed America. The ad was a plea to African-Americans not to listen to their own racists and separatists, but to embrace America's heritage with its creed that all men are created equal. What could be less racist than that? Yet without a second thought as to the damage it might inflict, Alter casually applied the stigma to me.

Alter's thoughtless attack reflected the double standards of the political culture that had shaped the debate, and that habitually tarred other conservative writers like Dinesh D'Souza and Ward Connerly without any regard for what they actually thought or wrote. *Washington Post* columnist Richard Cohen inadvertently illuminated the problem in an article devoted to the controversy, which he called "Specious Speech." Unlike Alter, Cohen not only defended the publication of the ad but also the argument itself, saying, "Word for word, the ad makes sense." Yet then he took away much of what he had just given when he also said the ad was guilty of being "offensive," as my critics had claimed: "But word for word is not, I learned a long time ago, how people read. They take in a message — a tone. The interior message of Horowitz's ad is smug, cold — dismissive. It's not racist, as some have charged. It just feels that way."[167]

The question that Cohen's article begged was this: Offensive to *whom?* My arguments were not directed at African-Americans, nor intended to dismiss their interests or feelings. My arguments were directed at partisans of a political idea that claimed that all America was guilty for the sins of slavery and that its poisons had continued into the present. Like others involved in the controversy over the ad, Cohen was finally unable to make the distinction between the political advocates of reparations, and the African-American community itself.

Long before I wrote the ad, black conservatives like Thomas Sowell and Walter Williams had made many of the arguments that appeared in it, including the most controversial one: that African-Americans owed

---

167. Richard Cohen, "Specious Speech," *Washington Post,* 22 March 2001.

a debt to their country.[168] The blunt tone I adopted was a response to the abrasive one my political opponents had used in making their case. It was also an homage to Sowell and Williams and other black conservatives for their courage under fire as their views were regularly stigmatized and dismissed by the same people. This was something that Cohen and the rest of my critics never considered.

Reparations advocates accuse America of being uniquely responsible for slavery; they ascribe malicious intent to every compromise with political reality; they deny America's achievement in ending slavery; they accuse every living citizen who is not black of benefiting from slavery and of being responsible for all economic disparities that black Americans suffer; they dismiss Americans' efforts in the realm of human rights and describe America as being "built on genocide, and theft, and slavery."[169] They accuse contemporary Americans of being "deeply, stubbornly, poisonously racist,"[170] and threaten that unless their demands are met, "America can have no future as one people."[171]

Are these statements *not* offensive? Yet who would publicly dare to say so? Who would take reparations advocates like Randall Robinson and Charles Ogletree to task for their hostility to America generally and to white Americans in particular? Of course, this is precisely what my ad did, and that is the reason for the reaction it provoked.

Randall Robinson, who is the leading spokesman for reparations, is certainly never criticized for *his* tone, which is often violent and inflammatory. His book *The Debt: What America Owes Blacks* has become the manifesto for the reparations cause, and he is a frequent spokesman before college audiences who always treat him with deference—an attitude shared by the nation's media.

In 1998, Robinson published an autobiography called *Defending the Spirit,* which chronicled a public career that had made him a national figure as a leader of the successful movement to impose economic sanctions on South Africa, a standing he has tried to transfer to the reparations issue. On the first page of his autobiography, Robinson informs the

---

168. Thomas Sowell, "Reparations for Slavery?" Creators Syndicate, 14 July 2000, www.townhall.com; Walter Williams, "Reparations for Slavery," Creators Syndicate, 12 July 2000, www.townhall.com; Walter Williams, "Does America Owe Reparations?" 7 February 2001, www.townhall.com. The idea that blacks alive today owed a debt to America was suggested by Sowell years ago.
169. Dorothy Benton-Lewis, MIT debate, 7 April 2001. http://video.C-Span.org:8080/ramgen/ndrive/e040701_slavery.rm.
170. Randall Robinson, *The Debt: What America Owes Blacks* (New York, 2000), p. 52.
171. Ibid., p. 208.

reader of his racial perspective: "I am obsessively black," he writes, and "race is an overarching aspect of my identity." But even this emotion is not his responsibility. "White Americans," Robinson claims, "have made me this way."[172] Two pages later he amplifies the confession: "White-hot hatred [of whites] would seem the proper reflex" for the "pain" that he feels. But prudence prevents him from expressing himself directly. As he puts it, "There is no survival there." Instead, he is forced into a muted self-reflection: "In the autumn of my life, I am left regarding white people, before knowing them individually, with irreducible mistrust and dull dislike."[173]

Robinson's attitude would inevitably be described as racist if confessed by a white writer. But in a black writer it is regarded as "gasp-out-loud frank,"[174] "provocative ... honest, bluntly told,"[175] "brutally frank"[176] and all in all "an unfiltered, uncensored, smart black voice in your ear." This last is the verdict pronounced on Robinson's book by Richard Cohen's paper, the *Washington Post*.

A page after confessing his obsession with race, Robinson offers the following reminiscence: "My father died in 1974 at the age of sixty-eight, of what the family now believes to have been Alzheimer's disease. Toward the end, and not lucid, he slapped a nurse, telling her not to 'put her white hands on him.' His illness had afforded him a final brief honesty. I was perversely pleased when told the story."[177] The honesty, along with the pleasure, evidently lies in the fact that his father's well-meaning helper was white and any gesture other than hostility towards a white person would be a lie.

The facts of Randall Robinson's life, as he relates them, make this bigotry difficult to comprehend, despite the fact that he was born in Richmond, Virginia, in the segregated South. Robinson's family was poor because of discrimination, although his father, Max, was a college graduate. When Randall was fourteen, the Supreme Court made its landmark decision to end segregation in the public schools. As a result of the changes that followed, the children of Max Robinson did better than he had. Much better. Randall's older brother, Max Jr., for example, became a famous

172. Randall Robinson, *Defending the Spirit: A Black Life in America* (New York, 1998), p.xiii.
173. Ibid., p. 1.
174. *Houston Chronicle*, quoted in front papers to *Defending the Spirit*.
175. *Raleigh News & Observer*, quoted in front papers to *Defending the Spirit*.
176. *Booklist*, quoted in front papers to *Defending the Spirit*.
177. Robinson, *Defending the Spirit*, p. 3.

newsman who eventually joined Peter Jennings as a co-anchor on ABC's *World News Tonight.*

The younger Randall was a poor student who went to Virginia Union University, a small college attended only by blacks. He dropped out of school before graduating to join the military, where in 1963 he was stationed at Fort Benning, Georgia. Just before his battalion was shipped overseas, a white army major with a "bluff manner" and a "voice [that] held a detectable trace of Old South money" encouraged Robinson to go back to school. The officer told him that if he applied to school he would be eligible for an early discharge, and he offered to expedite the application. That August, the major and his unit were shipped to Vietnam to fight one of the bloodiest engagements of the war. In September, Robinson returned to college. A month later, he recalls, "more than half of my former army battalion died in the battle of the Ia Drang Valley."[178]

Robinson graduated from his small black college and was recruited to Harvard Law School. Upon graduating from Harvard he decided not to become a lawyer, but to dedicate himself, as an activist, to the "empowerment and liberation of the African world." Over the years, his crusades brought him great material success, so that he was able to send his own teenage daughter to an exclusive $15,000-a-year private school while he pursued a public career, traveling to exotic locales around the world. In his own words, he "conferred with presidents, and more than once altered the course of American foreign policy."[179]

In his own lifetime, Randall Robinson witnessed the greatest revolution in race relations of any society in human history. He was born in 1940, in poverty, which was normal then for blacks, in the capital of the old slave South. Segregation was the law. This was before more than half of black America rose up from poverty and into the middle class. It was before the nation's military and schools and professional athletic leagues were integrated; before discrimination in government and business was outlawed; before a black could marry a white in many parts of the country; before a black American had served as the nation's military chief, a cabinet member in the White House, or a justice of the Supreme Court; before mayors and governors and more than six thousand elected officials from states all across America were black, many of them representing districts that are predominantly white. Yet for Randall Robinson, the American glass was not only not half full, but all the way empty: "I am convinced

---

178. Ibid., p. 53.
179. Ibid.

that I will die in a society as racially divided as the one into which I was born more than a half century ago."[180]

Bob Herbert, a black columnist for the *New York Times,* wrote: "*Defending the Spirit* [is] Mr. Robinson's account of his inability, despite a world-class education and tremendous professional success, to escape the humiliating trap of racism."[181] An anecdote at the beginning of the book captures what Herbert had in mind; it is told as a preface to the story of Max Robinson's final aggression.

In the spring of 1995, Robinson found himself "in back of a small country hardware store somewhere off Route 13 near Nassawadox on the Eastern Shore of Virginia." He had climbed onto a loading platform and was looking for the proprietor. As he did so, there were voices behind him. In front of the store, a young man in bib overalls was talking to another man who turned out to be the proprietor Robinson was seeking. "A boy jus went in theah looking fuh ya," the young man was saying in a thick southern drawl. The word "boy" stung Robinson, and the hurt grew worse when he realized he could not shake the rage he felt, even after the incident was past. Aware of his own elevated position in life, and the fact that the social disparities in the situation worked entirely in his favor, Robinson experienced a retrospective cognitive dissonance as he analyzed the event: "My rage is complicated by the balm of comparative material success. I tell myself that I cannot be wounded by a red-faced hayseed. But I am. The child lives on in the man until death."

Well, it does if you let it. The "insult," as Robinson describes it, seems motiveless and impersonal. Why react at all? It is a vestige of the past. But it is a past that Robinson keeps on exhuming until it assumes an aura so bright it manages to eclipse everything else: "The 'boy' to whom the semiliterate corn farmer is referring is I. And I have traveled a long way to nowhere."[182]

Nowhere? Can Randall Robinson—and Bob Herbert, who validates these sentiments—be serious? Robinson has traveled to places beyond anything his white irritant could imagine, and equally beyond the segregated poverty from which Robinson himself had emerged. If there is a wound here, it is self-inflicted. Robinson's view that his rage reflects the persistence of an inner child is certainly correct. But the remedy is to give up on the intellectual thumb sucking and grow up.

180. Ibid., p. xiv.
181. *New York Times,* 22 January, 1998.
182. Robinson, *Defending the Spirit,* p. 3.

Robinson and other upper-middle-class black intellectuals who hold on so obsessively to fantasies of racism would do well to recall the life of the African-American novelist Zora Neale Hurston, born fifty years before Robinson, who died in poverty after having to forge a career in the teeth of Jim Crow segregation. Hurston took an entirely different attitude to her racial harassers. In her lifetime, racial prejudices were not vestigial traces of a receding past, but the harsh mores and entrenched passions of the time itself. This, however, did not deter her. "Sometimes I feel discriminated against," Hurston wrote in 1927, "but it does not make me angry. It merely astonishes me. How can any deny themselves the pleasure of my company?"[183] Hurston even recognized advantages in her position as a racial underdog:

> No one on earth ever had a greater chance for glory. The world to be won and nothing to be lost. It is thrilling to think—to know that for any act of mine, I shall get twice as much praise or twice as much blame. It is quite exciting to hold the center of the national stage with the spectators not knowing whether to laugh or to weep. The position of my white neighbor is much more difficult. No brown specter pulls up a chair beside me when I sit down to eat. No dark ghost thrusts its leg against mine in bed. The game of keeping what one has is never so exciting as the game of getting.[184]

As a result of the changes that have taken place in America, the issue is less one of race than of perspective on race. The moral trumps, the laws, the institutions of power in American society are today all arrayed on the side of the "victims" in these dramas. Racism exists and racists persist, but they are irretrievably on the defensive. If W. E. B. Du Bois was right in saying that the problem of the twentieth century was the color line, it would also be correct to say that one of the problems of the twenty-first century will be the persistence of memories about that experience. In America, racism of the kind that provides Robinson a frisson of authenticity is an heirloom of the past. There is no war in the open that racists have the slightest hope of winning. There is racial injustice but it is injustice in the shadows. In America today, no racial prejudice, whether in institutions or individuals, can withstand exposure to the public light. That is the revolutionary transformation between the life spans of Randall Robinson and Zora Neale Hurston. In this millennium there is no reason to be a victim. But in order not to be one, you first have to stop thinking like one.

---

183. *The World Tomorrow,* May 1928, in *Zora Neale Hurston,* The Library of America (New York, 1995), p. 829.
184. Ibid., pp. 827–28.

REPARATIONS AND THE

AMERICAN IDEA

Someone is always at my elbow reminding me that I am the granddaughter of slaves. It fails to register depression with me. Slavery is sixty years in the past. The operation was successful and the patient is doing well, thank you. The terrible struggle that made me an American out of a potential slave said "On the line!" The Reconstruction said "Get set!" and the generation before said "Go!" I am off to a flying start and I must not halt in the stretch to look behind and weep. Slavery is the price I paid for civilization, and the choice was not with me. It is a bully adventure and worth all that I have paid through my ancestors for it.

Zora Neale Hurston, "How It Feels to Be Colored Me," 1927

I n making a case against reparations, I was taking sides on an issue that was integral to the "culture war," a schism that has polarized and embittered debate in America for nearly half a century. In part, this war reflects a nation divided over moral relativism and the issues of modernity. But it also derives from the battles of a Cold War that is not yet settled at home. My ad had stumbled into an argument over the meaning of American history and the nation's identity itself.

Since the 1960s, the "tenured radicals" have waged a ferocious assault on America's conception of itself as a beacon of freedom. Academic leftists have created a vast corpus of social theory that recasts old Marxist ideas in new "postmodern" molds and reinterprets the narrative of American freedom as a chronicle of race and class oppression. A nation conceived in liberty is newly described as "a nation conceived in slavery."[185] A "nation of immigrants" becomes a nation of victims. The reparations

---

185. James W. Loewen, *Lies My Teacher Told Me* (New York, 1996), p. 182. Loewen is a professor of sociology at the University of Vermont. Prominent left-wing historians who provided the scholarly basis for his revisionist text are Howard Zinn (*A People's History of the United States*), Ronald Takaki (*A Different Mirror*), Gary Nash (*Red, White and Black*), Francis Jennings (*The Invasion of America*), Kirkpatrick Sale (*The Conquest of Paradise*). Support for this hostile text was provided by two postdoctoral fellowships granted to Loewen by the Smithsonian Institution.

idea is a product of this historical revisionism. It has been designed by its advocates to refute America's self-image as a nation dedicated to equality of all and, in Abraham Lincoln's words, "the last best hope of mankind." It is because Lincoln and Jefferson are the indispensable shapers of this American idea, in fact, that they are also principal targets of the reparations left.

In its modern form, this movement was launched by a Sixties radical named James Forman in 1969. Forman interrupted a Sunday morning service at New York's Riverside Church to read a "Black Manifesto," which demanded $500 million from churches and synagogues as "a beginning of the reparations due us as people who have been exploited and degraded, brutalized, killed and persecuted."[186] Despite the favorable atmosphere of the time, the manifesto's demands remained then, and for many years after, the expression of a political fringe. No element of the civil rights leadership—neither the NAACP, nor the Urban League, nor the Congress for Racial Equality—took up Forman's claim.

During the next two decades, the issue remained isolated on the political margins. But in 1988, when Congress passed legislation to provide payment to Japanese-Americans who had been relocated for security reasons during World War II,[187] the reparations advocates saw an opening. The following year, Democrat congressman John Conyers introduced HR 40, a bill to create a commission parallel to the one that had paved the way for the Japanese. The bill was to "acknowledge the fundamental injustice, cruelty, brutality, and inhumanity of slavery in the United States and the 13 American colonies between 1619 and 1865 and to establish a commission to examine the institution of slavery, subsequent *de jure* and *de facto* racial and economic discrimination against African Americans, to make recommendations to the Congress on appropriate remedies, and for

---

186. James Forman, *The Making of Black Revolutionaries* (Seattle, 2000), pp. 343–52.
187. The decision to pay reparations to Japanese-Americans relocated for security reasons during World War II is a cautionary tale of what happens to issues of justice in an inflamed political environment. In fact, no Japanese-American was required to enter a relocation camp—only to leave coastal regions threatened by Japan. Many of those interned rejected oaths of allegiance to the United States, requested repatriation to Japan and organized political protests against the American war effort. In its decision to award reparations, Congress ignored the intelligence reports on which the relocation order was based, singling out only racial and ethnic prejudice among other factors, and made no distinction among the recipients as to whether they had actually obstructed the American war effort or were in fact a threat to security or were actually innocent of hostile intentions. Lowell Ponte, "Did Japanese-Americans in WW II Really Deserve Reparations?" www.frontpagemagazine.com, 2 July 2001.

other purposes."[188] Thirty-eight Democratic congressmen signed on as co-sponsors.

This moved the issue into the political mainstream. A decade later, the cause had won the support of leading black intellectuals and professionals, and by June 2001, Randall Robinson could accurately claim, "there is no major black organization that does not support reparations."[189]

This dramatic change in the attitude of black leadership can be attributed to changes that have taken place in the civil rights movement since the death of Martin Luther King. Under King's stewardship, the civil rights movement had pursued a quintessentially conservative goal: fulfilling the promise of equality in the American founding. It was a promise that first slavery, and then segregation and Jim Crow had thwarted, by denying full citizenship rights to black Americans. But after the passage of the Voting Rights Act and the elimination of legal discrimination in the 1960s, the civil rights movement confronted a dilemma.

The rights of African-Americans were now backed by the full power of the federal government. The next few years would see thousands of black elected officials, at all governmental levels. Black Americans were the heads of police departments and big city school administrations. Blacks had become the chief executives of major American cities—including New York, Los Angeles, Chicago, Detroit, Baltimore, Cleveland, Philadelphia, Atlanta, Houston, Washington, D.C., and even Selma, the symbol of segregation's last stand. There were no longer any institutional barriers to black progress that required legal redress. Within a generation, three-quarters of America's black population had risen out of poverty, and by the 1980s the black middle class would outnumber the black "underclass" for the first time in American history.[190] Public opinion polls began to register a seismic shift in white attitudes towards African-Americans on issues like integration and intermarriage, showing dramatic increases in levels of tolerance and social acceptance that had seemed unimaginable only a decade before King's triumph. These new attitudes were also reflected in the implementation of affirmative action programs designed "to redress past social injustices" and in massive government efforts to assist the underclass in which black Americans had been disproportionately represented.

188. Randall Robinson, *The Debt: What America Owes to Blacks* (New York, 2000), p. 201.
189. Tamar Lewin, "Calls for Slavery Restitution Getting Louder," *New York Times*, 4 June 2001.
190. This remarkable story is told in Stephan and Abigail Thernstrom, *America in Black and White* (New York, 1997).

But despite all these successes, a significant segment of the black community continued to lag behind, and the problem of racial "gaps" did not go away. Inequalities in education, economic status and criminal incarceration rates persisted, and their persistence confronted black leadership with a crisis of identity and purpose. It was in their resolution of this crisis that post-King civil rights leaders found a direction that inexorably brought them to the reparations cause.

In explaining the remaining gaps, civil rights leaders (or "professionals," as some were beginning to call them) turned to "continuing American racism" as the root cause of these intractable disparities. The explanation served to relieve those African-Americans who had fallen behind of the burden of accountability, while any other perspective was quickly dismissed as "blaming the victim." Martin Luther King himself had resisted this racial determinism—as even his most eloquent rival, Malcolm X, had done. "We know that there are many things wrong in the white world," King said, "but there are many things wrong in the black world, too. We can't keep on blaming the white man. There are things we must do for ourselves."[191]

Shelby Steele has described the determinist doctrine of King's successors as a "totalist" view. In a "totalist" perspective, "victimization" explains both "the hard fate of blacks in American history" and also "the current inequalities between blacks and whites and the difficulties blacks have in overcoming them."[192] But people also suffer, as Steele observed, "from bad ideas, from ignorance, fear, a poor assessment of reality and from a politics that commits them to the idea of themselves as victims." When the idea that people are agents of their fate is replaced with the idea that they are merely objects, that "*all* suffering is victimization," the inevitable conclusion is that relief comes from outside—from "the guilty good-heartedness of others."[193] This is the malign symbiosis at the heart of the reparations idea.

"The yawning economic gap between whites and blacks in this country ... was opened by the 246 year practice of slavery," Randall Robinson declares in *The Debt*. "It has been resolutely nurtured since in law and public policy. It has now ossified. It is structural. Its framing beams are disguised only by the counterfeit manners of a hypocritical governing class."[194]

---

191. Quoted in Jason L. Riley, "Don't Replace Jesse Jackson," *Wall Street Journal*, 18 April 2001. W. E. B. Du Bois had a similar attitude.
192. Shelby Steele, *A Dream Deferred: The Second Betrayal of Black Freedom in America* (New York, 1998), p. 10.
193. Ibid. Emphasis in original.
194. Robinson, *The Debt*, p. 204. Americans, he writes, must first "accept that the gap derives from the social depredations of slavery." Ibid., p. 173.

Every element of Robinson's totalist thesis is specious. Does Robinson really believe that before the arrival of slaves in Jamestown, there was *no* economic gap between Europeans who lived in an era of nascent capitalism and scientific revolution, and Africans whose preliterate tribal cultures were still mired in the Bronze Age? After billions were spent on affirmative action programs, federal anti-discrimination laws and extensive social programs aimed at addressing racial barriers and deficits, how is it possible to say that the gap between blacks and whites has been "resolutely nurtured" for the last 136 years? And what exactly is indicated by the gap itself? As Thomas Sowell has observed, scholars have studied racial and ethnic groups around the world and have not come up with a single country where all the different groups have the same incomes and occupations. "Why would people from Africa be the lone exception on this planet? Groups everywhere differ too much in too many ways to have the same outcomes."[195]

The length to which Robinson is willing to take his "totalism"—the idea that the life of every black person in America can be explained in terms of victimization by whites—is apparently without limit: "What can we say to the black man on death row? The black mother alone, bitter, overburdened and spent? Who tells them that their fate washed ashore at Jamestown with twenty slaves in 1619?"[196]

These sentences seem to imply that a black murderer in the twenty-first century commits his crime because his ancestors were dragged to America in chains. Is Robinson aware of how absurd this sounds, and how insulting it is to the vast majority of black Americans who are descended from slaves and law-abiding as well?

The view that every disparity African-Americans may experience is a legacy of slavery and white racism is shared, in fact, by all reparations proponents and is the basis of their planned lawsuit against the United States Government. Harvard law professor Charles Ogletree is head of the Reparations Coordinating Committee, a team of high-powered class action lawyers who are designing the legal action. When asked by a reporter why he thought the government should pay reparations, Ogletree said: "It's been 250 years of slavery, 100 years of Jim Crow legal segregation and we have not fully addressed or remedied the 350 years of direct suffering that African-Americans have endured in the United States." Asked what he thought some of the lingering effects of slavery were, Ogletree

195. Thomas Sowell, "Reparations for Slavery," Creators Syndicate, 14 July 2000. Sowell himself is probably the leading academic expert on the subject.
196. Robinson, *The Debt*, pp. 216–17.

replied: "Racial profiling, selective incarceration, disparate sentencing, inner city poverty, limited opportunities, the whole issue of economic inequality, substandard health care and other life-threatening health issues. Discriminatory lending practices, redlining, and a host of other issues that are directly related to race. They are as apparent in the twenty-first century as they were in the seventeenth century."[197]

To read the statements of reparations advocates is to realize that they invoke slavery not as a dark episode in the American past, but as an emblem of contemporary America. In a response to my appearance at Arizona State University, Professor Michael Eric Dyson told students: "[Americans] can't talk about slavery because it indicts the American soul."[198] An indictment of the American soul is the subtext of every argument in behalf of the reparations claim.

Thus Robinson's manifesto begins with the following declaration: "This book is about the great *still-unfolding* massive crime of official and unofficial America against Africa, African slaves, and their descendants in America" (emphasis added).[199] Throughout *The Debt*, the theme is pounded home: "At long last, let America contemplate the scope of its enduring human-rights wrong against the whole of a people. Let the vision of blacks not become so blighted from a sunless eternity that we fail to see the staggering breadth of America's crime against us."[200] The "enormous human rights crime of slavery (later practiced as peonage)," Robinson elaborates, "[has been] overlapped and extended by a century of government-sponsored segregation and general racial discrimination." While black Americans suffered, the white American masters reaped the rewards of that suffering: "Of course, benefiting inter-generationally from this weather of racism were white Americans whose assets piled up like fattening snowballs over three and a half centuries' terrain of slavery and the mean racial climate that followed it."[201]

Robinson's assessment of the scope of America's malignancy is boundless: "The enslavement of blacks in America lasted 246 years. It was

---

197. Interview with Alex Kellogg, BET.com, 11 April 2001. Cf. AP, 5 November 2000.
198. Kevin Grant, "Socialist Professor Addresses Student Audience on Reparations and Race Relations," *Arizona State Press*, 24 April 2001. Dyson, a leading African American intellectual, is a professor at DePaul University and was flown in at University expense for the rebuttal. He is the author of books on Malcolm X and Martin Luther King Jr. and the honorary co-chair of the Democratic Socialists of America.
199. Robinson, *The Debt*, p. 8.
200. Ibid., p. 9.
201. Ibid.. pp. 226, 227.

followed by a century of legal racial segregation and discrimination. The two periods, taken together, constitute the longest running crime against humanity in the world over the last 500 years."[202]

Greater than the Nazi Holocaust, the Soviet gulag, the Armenian genocide, the Cambodian killing fields, the nightmare in Rwanda, or the slave system in Africa itself!

In fact, Africa's *internal* slave trade, which did not involve the United States or any European power, not only extended over the entire 500 years mentioned by Robinson, but also preceded it by nearly 1,000 years. In the period between 650 and 1600, *before* any Western involvement, somewhere between 3 million and 10 million Africans were bought by Muslim slavers for use in Saharan societies and in the trade in the Indian Ocean and the Red Sea.[203] By contrast, the enslavement of blacks in the United States lasted 89 years, from 1776 until 1865. The combined slave trade to the British colonies in North America and later to the United States accounted for less than 3 percent of the global trade in African slaves. The total number of slaves imported to North America was 800,000, less than the slave trade to the island of Cuba alone. If the *internal* African slave trade—which began in the seventh century and persists to this day in the Sudan, Mauritania and other sub-Saharan states—is taken into account, the responsibility of American traders shrinks to a fraction of 1 percent of the slavery problem.[204]

In sum, even taking into account the millions of slaves born in North America,[205] America's role in the global tragedy of slave systems involving

202. This statement was made at a TransAfrica reparations forum attended by the chief counsel for the National Coalition of Blacks for Reparations in America; a representative of the NAACP Legal Defense and Educational Fund; William Fletcher, assistant to the president of the AFL-CIO; Dorothy Height, chair of the National Council of Negro Women; Wade Henderson, executive director, Leadership Conference on Civil Rights; John Conyers; Charles Ogletree; and professors Charles Lawrence and Mari Matsuda (the legal architects of campus speech codes). The forum was broadcast on C-Span. The transcript is available at www.transafricaforum.org/reports/print/reparations_print.shtml.
203. Paul Lovejoy, *Transformations in Slavery: A History of Slavery in Africa* (Cambridge, 2000), p. 25.
204. Robert Fogel, *Without Consent or Contract: The Rise and Fall of American Slavery* (New York, 1994), p.7. Thomas Sowell, *Race and Culture* (New York, 1994), p. 188: "Over the centuries, somewhere in the neighborhood of 11 million people were shipped across the Atlantic from Africa as slaves, and another 14 million African slaves were taken across the Sahara Desert or shipped through the Persian Gulf and other waterways to the nations of North Africa and the Middle East."
205. There were an estimated 800,000 slaves imported, but a slave population of four million in the United States by 1860.

Africans, while bad enough, was relatively minor compared with the roles of Arabs, Europeans and Africans themselves.

Robinson's attempt to expand America's responsibility for these tragedies by including segregation and discrimination as "crimes against humanity" reveals far more about the maker of the claim than its target. To minimize injustices suffered by innumerable minorities the world over—let alone the genocides of Cambodians, Rwandans, Armenians, Jews and others during the five-hundred-year period Robinson cites—is to diminish the enormity of those crimes merely to justify a personal hostility towards the United States.

That this hostility, rather than a desire for justice, is what animates the reparations movement was clear in my MIT debate with Dorothy Benton-Lewis, when she summed up her views in this terse and crude formulation: "Slavery and white supremacy are alive and well in America and the issue of reparations is about dealing with the truth and exposing this country for what it is."[206] *For what it is.* I realized after the furor had begun that challenging this slander was the chief offense of my campus ad campaign.

What reparations supporters most roundly condemned were the ad's reminders of the contributions Americans have made to the cause of human freedom—and therefore to the freedom of African-Americans themselves. They do not want to hear this. For the same reason, a prominent feature of their arguments is an attack on the American Founders and the framework they created. "George Washington is not *my* ancestor, private or public," proclaims Randall Robinson to make the point as bluntly as possible. Washington was a slaveholder; in Robinson's view this is more important than anything else he may have done, including his decision to free his slaves. Yet that decision obviously said more about the nature of the man than his decision to have slaves in the first place, since it went against the grain of his culture, his region and his time.

But the most venomous rage in *The Debt* is reserved for Thomas Jefferson, the author of the document that put the promise of equality at the very center of the American idea. It is *because* Jefferson is the author of the words "all men are created equal" that Robinson and other reparations advocates feel compelled to attack him. "Jefferson," writes Robinson, "was a slaveholder, a racist and—if one accepts that consent cannot be given if it cannot be denied—a rapist."[207]

---

206. April 7, 2001. http://video.C-span.org:8080/ramgen/ndrive/e040701_slavery.rm.
207. Robinson, *The Debt*, p. 52.

Robinson is alluding to Jefferson's alleged sexual liaison with his slave Sally Hemings. It is possible that Jefferson did have such a relationship, but there is no incontrovertible evidence to establish this as a fact. The closest historians have come in linking Jefferson sexually to Hemings is DNA evidence that shows a Jefferson male to have fathered one of her children. But Thomas Jefferson was not the only male family member who enjoyed the proximity and had the opportunity to do so.[208] Even if he did father the ancestor of Eston Hemings, there is no basis whatsoever for Robinson's accusation that Sally Hemings was "raped." The very premise of Robinson's allegation is false, since, contrary to his assertion, consent *can* be given even in circumstances where it cannot be denied. Hemings could have been in love with Jefferson despite the fact that she was his slave. And vice versa. Such hazards of the human heart are obliterated in the ideologically flattened-out and spiteful world Robinson inhabits.

To press his indictment to the full, Robinson adds a gratuitous afterthought, suggesting that Jefferson "could have killed Sally and faced no consequences." The statement only reveals his ignorance of slavery in America—a complex rather than a simple reality. The Founders generally and Jefferson in particular did not regard slaves merely as property and—as I have already noted—even states of the Deep South, like North Carolina, made the murder of slaves by their owners a punishable crime. In *Federalist No. 54,* published the year the Constitution was adopted, James Madison wrote:

> We must deny the fact, that slaves are considered merely as property, and in no respect whatever as persons. The true state of the case is, that they partake of both these qualities: being considered by our laws, in some respects, as persons, and in other respects as property. In being compelled to labor, not for himself, but for a master; in being vendible by one master to another master; and in being subject at all times to be restrained in his liberty and chastised in his body, by the capricious will of another, the slave may appear to be degraded from the human rank, and classed with those irrational animals which fall under the legal denomination of property. *In being protected, on the other hand, in his life and in his limbs, against the violence of all others, even the*

---

208. Another family suspect, Jefferson's brother Randolph, was known to have spent time in the slave quarters at Monticello. Scholars have been able to place him at the estate at the times Sally was impregnated. Still Jefferson cannot be excluded as the possible father of Eston's ancestor. A prudent attitude would be to suspend judgment. Cf. "The Jefferson-Hemings Scholars Commission Report," 12 April 2001, http://www.mindspring.com/-tjshcommisson/. The commission exonerated Jefferson. The above information is taken from the lone dissent by historian Paul Rahe.

master of his labor and his liberty; and in being punishable himself
for all violence committed against others, the slave is no less evidently
regarded by the law as a member of the society, not as a part of the
irrational creation; as a moral person, not as a mere article of prop-
erty.[209] [emphasis added]

Robinson's attack, which must ignore these subtleties in order to press ahead with such ferocity, betrays his agenda, which is to attack America itself: "Does not the continuing un-remarked deification of Jefferson tell us all how profoundly contemptuous of black sensibilities American society persists in being? How deeply, stubbornly, poisonously racist our society to this day remains?"[210]

The statement is neither syntactically nor logically sound. In reality, the reverence for Jefferson tells us nothing about white America's attitudes towards black feelings, or about the alleged racism of American society. But it does reveal a lot about Randall Robinson's resentments. Over a century ago, the emancipated slave Frederick Douglass, one of the greatest of black leaders, made a profoundly different assessment of Jefferson and the Founders:

> The anti-slavery movement has little to entitle it to being called a new thing under the sun.... The patriots of the American Revolution clearly saw, and with all their inconsistency, they had the grace to confess the abhorrent character of slavery, and to hopefully predict its overthrow and complete extirpation. Washington and Jefferson, Patrick Henry and Luther Martin, Franklin, and Adams, Madison and Monroe, and a host of the earlier statesmen, jurists, scholars and divines of the country, were among those who looked forward to this happy consummation.[211]

In its honesty, Douglass's perspective links the destiny of former slaves with America's aspirations, which is precisely the vision that anti-American ideologues like Robinson seek to subvert.

The fierce hatred of Robinson and other reparations spokesmen for the author of the *Declaration of Independence* is paralleled by a similar antipathy towards the architect of emancipation and the "second American

---

209. 12 February 1788. I am grateful to Thomas West for this reference. In the same *Federalist,* Madison characterized as "barbarous" the policy of treating other human beings as property.
210. Robinson, *The Debt,* p. 52.
211. Philip S. Foner, ed. *Frederick Douglass: Selected Speeches and Writings* (New York, 1999), p. 314.

founding"—Abraham Lincoln. The intellectual leadership of this assault has fallen to historian Lerone Bennett Jr., who is also the executive editor of the leading popular black magazine, *Ebony*. Bennett was one of three witnesses to testify at the hearings preceding the Chicago City Council resolution on reparations. He told the council that American slavery was "the greatest crime in human history."[212]

Recently, *Ebony*'s publishing company, which is the largest black publishing empire in America, released a 600-page crank history by Bennett called *Forced into Glory: Abraham Lincoln's White Dream*. It presents the full-blown treatment of a thesis Bennett has been advocating in the pages of *Ebony* for more than three decades. He claims that Abraham Lincoln was a racist and a fraud (because he pretended to free the slaves) and that "Lincoln must be seen as the embodiment, not the transcendence, of the American tradition of racism."[213]

Ironically, Bennett's view of Lincoln is shared by the right-wing polemicist Joseph Sobran and the intellectuals grouped around the Conservative Citizens Council. They regard Lincoln as a racist tyrant who conducted an illegal war against the South while privately maintaining views of Negro inequality that made his proclamations (and deeds) to the contrary hypocritical. Sobran has been criticized by conservatives like Jack Kemp for being one of the current "assassins of Lincoln's character" and is at work on his own book, *King Lincoln*. While praising Bennett's *Forced into Glory* for showing that the image of Lincoln as a "cherished crusader for equality—is a wholly imaginary being," Sobran has acknowledged that he has been able to add "only a few salient details" to Bennett's own hatchet job.[214]

The views of Bennett and Sobran stand in stark contrast to the testimony of Frederick Douglass, who visited Lincoln in the White House and was struck by the president's "freedom from popular prejudice against the colored people. He was the first great man that I talked with in the United States freely, who in no single instance reminded me of the difference between himself and myself, of the difference of color."[215]

212. "Politicians, Scholars Voice Support for Slavery Reparation," *Jetonline!* 15 May 2000. Another witness was Congressman Bobby Rush, former head of the Black Panther Party in Chicago.

213. Lerone Bennett, *Forced into Glory: Abraham Lincoln's White Dream* (Chicago, 2000). Bennett comes to this conclusion by a sustained wrenching of Lincoln's statements and actions out of their historical context, completely ignoring the complex political coalition Lincoln had to lead to achieve emancipation.

214. "The Imaginary Abe," *Sobran's,* www.sobran.com/replyJaffa.shtml.

215. Foner, *Frederick Douglass,* pp. 546–47.

A cardinal complaint of the reparations partisans is the claim that "this country has never dealt with slavery," or confronted its evil, as Charles Ogletree put it.[216] But, in fact, America *has* dealt with slavery, in the course of its bloodiest and most soul-wrenching conflict—a Civil War in which Americans put the very existence of their nation at risk to do so. And it dealt with it again in the so-called Second Civil War of the civil rights movement, when individuals—white as well as black—put their lives on the line precisely to deal once and for all with the legacy of slavery.

The present government of the United States, which the reparations lawyers propose to hold culpable for the crime of slavery, is lineally descended from the government that fought and bore the costs of the war that ended slavery. The recognition that slavery was a moral evil was the ultimate cause of that war, although reparations advocates argue tendentiously that the Civil War was "not about slavery," but only about "saving the Union" and "economic interests." (The same people who make this claim, however, do not say that the Confederate battle flag should be removed from public buildings because it is a symbol of "economic interests.") The claim cannot withstand historical scrutiny.

From its very inception as a nation, America's Founders understood that the creed of liberty and equality, which had inspired its creation, inevitably brought it into collision with the system of human bondage it had inherited from the British Empire. In the Jefferson Memorial these words are enshrined:

> God who gave us life gave us liberty. Can the liberties of a nation be secure when we have removed a conviction that these liberties are the gift of God? Indeed I tremble for my country when I reflect that God is just, that his justice cannot sleep forever. Commerce between Master and slave is despotism. Nothing is more certainly written in the book of fate than that these people are to be free.

The words "slave" and "black" do not appear in the Constitution because the Framers believed that slavery was a dying and immoral institution and they did not want to recognize it more than absolutely necessary to achieve the compromise with the southern colonies that they considered vital to the survival of the Republic.[217] As Lincoln put it in 1854, "the thing is hid away in the Constitution, just as an afflicted man hides away a wen or a cancer, which he dares not cut out at once, lest he bleed

216. Interview with Alex Kellogg, BET.com, 11 April 2001.
217. The dilemmas of the Founders are elegantly explored in chapter 3 ("The Silence") of Joseph Ellis's *The Founding Brothers* (New York, 2000).

to death; with the promise, nevertheless, that the cutting may begin at the end of a given time."[218] Beyond ending the slave trade, which they did in 1808, the Founders had no practical idea—short of a war between the states—of how to abolish the institution itself.[219]

The flawed compromise with slavery in the American founding was the inescapable subtext of the national debates that led up to the war: whether liberty could or should be compromised in fugitive slave laws; whether the terrain of freedom should or should not be extended in the addition of new states; whether a nation could endure half slave and half free. In 1861, these questions were answered in a fratricidal resolution.

No figure in American politics so personified America's encounter with itself over the moral issue of slavery as its Civil War president, Abraham Lincoln. No political leader formulated the connection of slavery to the national issue so eloquently as Lincoln in the pre-war debates with Senator Stephen Douglas:

> Our progress in degeneracy appears to be pretty rapid [Lincoln argued in 1855]. As a nation we began by declaring that, "all men are created equal." We now practically read it "all men are created equal, except Negroes." When the Know-Nothings get control, it will read "all men are created equal, except Negroes, and foreigners, and Catholics." When it comes to this I should prefer emigrating to some other country where they make no pretence of loving liberty—to Russia, for instance, where despotism can be taken pure without the base alloy of hypocrisy.[220]

As political scientist Harry V. Jaffa has summarized Lincoln's pre-war role in this conflict, "the assertion of equality in the Declaration of Independence was the prop and pillar of the antislavery cause. One might epitomize everything Lincoln said between 1854 and 1861 as a demand for recognition of the Negro's human rights, as set forth in the Declaration."[221]

---

218. James McPherson, *Abraham Lincoln and the Second American Revolution* (New York, 1991), p. 126.
219. The rationales for the compromise are laid out in Ellis, *The Founding Brothers*.
220. Cited in McPerson, *Abraham Lincoln*, p. 53. This small classic is the best introduction to the singular role that Lincoln played in freeing the slaves. Contrary views are invariably based on reading individual presidential statements or acts out of context, and failing to understand the complexities of the coalition Lincoln was leading or the perilous situation of the northern cause at various stages of the conflict. McPherson's account admirably sets the record straight.
221. Harry V. Jaffa, *A New Birth of Freedom: Abraham Lincoln and the Coming of the Civil War* (Lanham, Md., 2000), p. 74.

It was the election, in 1860, of the man who held such views that triggered the secession of seven slave states and the formation of the Confederacy. The president of the Confederacy, Jefferson Davis, explained secession as an effort "to save ourselves from a revolution" that threatened to make "property in slaves so insecure as to be comparatively worthless."[222] The slaves themselves concurred, according to the testimony of Booker T. Washington:

> During the campaign when Lincoln was first a candidate for the Presidency, the slaves on our far-off plantation, miles from any railroad or large city or daily newspaper, knew what the issues involved were. When war was begun between the North and the South, every slave on our plantation felt and knew that, though other issues were discussed, the primal one was that of slavery. Even the most ignorant members of my race on the remote plantations felt that the freedom of the slaves would be the one great result of the war, if the Northern armies conquered.[223]

Dismissed by reparations partisans as a mere expediency to win the war, the Emancipation Proclamation was in fact the fulfillment of a design Lincoln had long held, but which political circumstances prevented him from implementing earlier. Lincoln's was one of four parties contesting the election. Four border states that were crucial to the Union cause were slave states. Lincoln could not have put together—or maintained—the coalition that won the war had he defined it as an anti-slavery cause at the outset. For the same reason, the Emancipation Proclamation extended freedom only to slaves rebelling against the Confederacy. Preserving the Union was the war aim that united the coalition. But as the war progressed, Lincoln steadily redefined the Union war aims even as he redefined the American covenant and its "charter of freedom."

At Gettysburg, Lincoln declared the war a test to see "whether a nation conceived in liberty and dedicated to the proposition that all men are created equal" could endure. He proclaimed the war "a new birth of freedom," and identified the new freedom and the Union cause with the emancipation of the slaves. "Let us re-adopt the Declaration of Independence, and with it the practices and policy which harmonize it," Lincoln had said in the last debate with Douglas, before the first shot was fired.

---

222. Cited in McPherson, *Abraham Lincoln*, p. 27.
223. Booker T. Washington, *Up from Slavery* (New York, 2000), pp. 5–6.

"If we do this, we shall not only have saved the Union; but we shall have so saved it, as to make, and keep it, forever worthy of the saving."[224]

Far from officially ignoring the evil of slavery or the need for reparation, Lincoln described the war itself as God's form of retribution—a payment in blood for the sins committed against African slaves. In 1864, in his Second Inaugural Address, he said:

> American slavery is one of those offences which, in the providence of God ... He now wills to remove [through] this terrible war, as the woe due to those whom the offence came.... Fondly do we hope— fervently do we pray—that this mighty scourge of war may speedily pass away. Yet if God wills that it continue, until all the wealth piled by the bondman's two hundred and fifty years of unrequited toil shall be sunk, and until every drop of blood drawn with the lash, shall be paid by another drawn with the sword, as was said three thousand years ago, so still it must be said "the judgments of the Lord, are true and righteous altogether."[225]

To make their rancid case against Lincoln, Bennett and other reparations partisans ignore the human context of Lincoln's struggle with (as much as against) slavery. They suck the marrow out of a complex and ultimately heroic human drama, just as they do when they ignore the weight and consequence of Washington's freeing of his slaves. The Civil War was, as Frederick Douglass said, "the abolition war," and no one has summed up Lincoln's calculation and achievement in successfully managing it better than Douglass himself:

> His great mission was to accomplish two things: first, to save his country from dismemberment and ruin; and, second, to free his country from the great crime of slavery. To do one or the other, or both, he must have the earnest sympathy and the powerful cooperation of his loyal fellow-countrymen. Without this primary and essential condition to success, his efforts must have been vain and utterly fruitless. Had he put the abolition of slavery before the salvation of the Union, he would have inevitably driven from him a powerful class of the American people and rendered resistance to rebellion impossible. Viewed from the genuine abolition ground, Mr. Lincoln seemed tardy, cold, dull, and indifferent; but measuring him by the sentiment of his

---

224. McPherson, *Abraham Lincoln*, p. 55. The evolution of Lincoln's political strategy with respect to slavery is outlined in this book.
225. Second Inaugural Address, 4 March 1864, *The Essential Abraham Lincoln*, ed. John Gabriel Hunt (New York, 1993), p. 331.

country, a sentiment he was bound as a statesman to consult, he was swift, zealous, radical, and determined. Though Mr. Lincoln shared the prejudices of his white fellow-countrymen against the Negro, it is hardly necessary to say that in his heart of hearts he loathed and hated slavery.[226]

More Americans died in the Civil War than in all other wars involving Americans combined. John Brown had said that the sin of slavery made it necessary to "purge this land with blood." More than 350,000 Americans lost their lives in the northern armies that vanquished the slave power. Was this not a form of atonement?

When the economic and human costs of the war are added up, much—if not all—of the national wealth said to have been accumulated through slavery was spent or destroyed in the war that ended it. Retributive justice was ruthlessly exacted on the South:

> When the Civil War became a total war the invading army intentionally destroyed the economic capacity of the South to wage war. Union armies ripped up thousands of miles of southern railroads and blew up hundreds of bridges.... More than half of the South's farm machinery was wrecked by the war, two-fifths of its livestock were slaughtered, and one-quarter of its white males of military age—also the prime age for economic production—were killed, a higher proportion than suffered by any European power in World War I, that holocaust which ravaged a continent and spread revolution through many of its countries.

The war destroyed 60 percent of southern wealth and "the value of southern agricultural land in relation to that of the North was cut by three-fourths."[227]

These historical realities completely refute the reparations claims that slavery was never confronted and a price was never paid. The Civil War was indeed a second American Revolution. It not only redefined the founding covenant, making America the first multiracial nation in the world, but it was also a revolution in the strict sense, overthrowing the power of the slaveholding class. As a result of the war, the political supremacy of this class was destroyed. Thanks to the durability of the "Virginia Dynasty," the president of the United States had been a southerner

---

226. Foner, *Frederick Douglass*, p. 621.
227. McPherson, *Abraham Lincoln*, p. 38.

and a slaveholder for 49 of the nation's first 72 years. After the war, it was a century before another southerner was elected to the White House. Before the war, 23 of 36 Speakers of the House of Representatives had been southerners and 24 of 36 presidents *pro tem* of the Senate. For the next fifty years no southerner was elected leader of either chamber. Until the Civil War, the South had a majority on the Supreme Court every year. But during the next half-century, only 5 of 26 justices were southerners.[228] As a result of the war, the power of the southern plantocracy that had forced the three-fifths compromise and the fugitive slave clause and was responsible for the Dred Scott decision was destroyed.

This is the answer to the arguments of reparations advocates like columnist Earl Ofari Hutchinson. "The U.S. government, not long dead Southern planters, bears the blame for slavery," Hutchinson wrote. "It encoded it in the Constitution in Article One. This designated a black slave as three-fifths of a person for tax and political representation purposes. It protected and nourished it in Article Four by mandating that all escaped slaves found anywhere in the nation be returned to their masters. In the Dred Scott decision in 1857, the U.S. Supreme Court reaffirmed that slaves remained slaves no matter where they were taken in the United States."[229] But the planter class guilty of those crimes was extinguished in 1865. What is the rationale for holding the vanquisher liable for the sins of the vanquished?

Hyperbolic indictments of America have become such routine features of the political landscape that they have begun to eclipse the memory of the attitudes they displaced—attitudes once expressed by former slaves like Booker T. Washington:

> Think about it: we went into slavery pagans; we came out Christians. We went into slavery pieces of property; we came out American citizens. We went into slavery with chains clanking about our wrists; we came out with the American ballot in our hands.... When we rid ourselves of prejudice, or racial feeling, and look the facts in the face, we must acknowledge that, notwithstanding the cruelty and moral wrong of slavery, we are in a stronger and more hopeful position, materially, intellectually, morally, and religiously, than is true of an equal number of black people in any other portion of the globe.[230]

■   ■

---

228. Ibid., p. 13.
229. Earl Ofari Hutchinston, "10 Reasons Why Reparations Is a Good Idea for Americans, and Horowitz Too," *Salon.com*, 30 March 2001.
230. Booker T. Washington, *Up from Slavery*, p. 11. Cf. also John Perazzo, *The Myths That Divide Us* (1998), p. 377.

The case for reparations is an attack not only on Abraham Lincoln and all he symbolized but on post–Civil War America. The refusal of President Andrew Johnson to honor the promise of "40 acres and a mule" to freed slaves when the war concluded was certainly an injustice—and a costly one. So were the injuries inflicted by segregation and discrimination. When the Civil Rights Acts of the 1960s finally established full citizenship for black Americans, the government had a clear obligation to devise programs that would attempt to repair injuries these injustices had inflicted. The government—with the support of the American public—did just that.

Yet reparations partisans will deny it. Given their totalist view, the denial is probably inevitable: Why should racist Americans suddenly manifest good intentions, when for the previous two hundred years they had not? Thus Randall Robinson dismisses the efforts of the War on Poverty, the Great Society, and the Nixon affirmative action programs with an impatient gesture: "In 1965, after nearly 350 years of legal racial suppression, the United States enacted the Voting Rights Act and, virtually simultaneously, began to walk away from the social wreckage that centuries of white hegemony had wrought."[231]

The statement is utterly false. Since Robinson can hardly be ignorant of this history, his dismissal merely betrays the animus that lies behind his case. On June 4, 1965—just shy of a hundred years since the Emancipation Proclamation—President Lyndon Johnson gave a famous commencement address at Howard University, vetted in advance by civil rights leaders, in which he described the vision inspiring his War on Poverty and Great Society programs. In this speech he made explicit—and official—the special obligation Americans had to make up for past injustices committed against black citizens:

> This is the next and the more profound stage of the battle for civil rights. We seek not just freedom but opportunity. We seek not just legal equity but human ability, not just equality as a right and a theory but equality as a fact and equality as a result. For the task is to give 20 million Negroes the same chance as every other American to learn and grow, to work and share in society, to develop their abilities—physical, mental and spiritual, and to pursue their individual happiness.[232]

Freedom was "not enough," said President Johnson. "You do not wipe away the scars of centuries by saying: Now you are free to go where

---

231. Robinson, *The Debt,* p. 230.
232. "To Fulfill These Rights," http://www.lbjlib.utexas.edu/johnson/archives.hom/speeches.hom650604.htm.

you want, and do as you desire.... You do not take a person who, for years has been hobbled by chains and liberate him, bring him up to the starting line of a race and then say... 'you are free to compete with all the others,' and still justly believe that you have been completely fair." This understanding was to become the rationale for "affirmative action" policies and all the racial preference programs for jobs, school placements and contract set-asides that would transfer billions of dollars of wealth to black citizens over the next three decades.

But in the Howard speech Johnson also used the same terms to describe the anti-poverty welfare programs he set in motion. "For Negro poverty is not white poverty," he said; the differences between them were "not racial differences."[233] As if writing in advance the script later followed by Robinson and the reparations proponents,[234] he explained:

> They are solely and simply the consequence of ancient brutality, past injustice, and present prejudice. They are anguishing to observe. For the Negro they are a constant reminder of oppression. For the white they are a constant reminder of guilt. But they must be faced and they must be dealt with and they must be overcome, if we are ever to reach the time when the only difference between Negroes and whites is the color of their skin.

Johnson concluded his vision of "the next and the more profound stage of the battle for civil rights" by setting it in its historical frame: "So it is the glorious opportunity of this generation to end the one huge wrong of the American Nation."

In other words, nearly forty years ago the American government set out on exactly the path of repairing the wrong of slavery and its legacies, an effort that Robinson and the reparationists stubbornly deny was ever attempted.[235]

---

233. Compare Robinson: "Lamentably, there will always be poverty. But African Americans are overrepresented in that economic class for one reason and one reason only: American slavery and the vicious climate that followed it." *The Debt*, pp. 8–9.
234. "High infant mortality. Low income. High unemployment. Substandard education. Capital incapacity. Insurmountable credit barriers. High morbidity. Below-average life span. Overrepresentation in prison—and on death row. Each a cause and/or a consequence of disabling poverty—of means and spirit—that has shackled all too many entire black family trees since the Emancipation Proclamation.... Of the many reasons for this inequality, chief of course is the seemingly incurable virus of de facto discrimination that continues to poison relations between the races at all levels." Ibid., p. 62.
235. "Those who exercise control over our public policy see no reason why they should care very much about taking steps to fix what America has done to blacks." Ibid., p. 238.

During those years, trillions of dollars were spent in means-tested poverty programs under the Great Society welfare programs. These monies represented a *net* transfer of more than $1.3 trillion to African-Americans.[236] Johnson thought that the various gaps between black and white incomes could be closed by external means, that the problem of lagging black indices came from being "buried under a blanket of history and circumstance." Subsequent experience has proven him wrong. The welfare programs devised by well-intentioned social reformers not only did not reduce black poverty, but exacerbated and deepened it.[237] This reality poses questions that the reparations claimants do not even begin to address. If huge sums of government monies already expended have not made a dent in the solution to these problems, why should there be any cause to think "reparations" might solve them in the future?

Johnson's initiative in expanding the welfare state and in directing anti-poverty efforts to inner-city areas with large concentrations of African-Americans[238] was followed by Richard Nixon's reinvention of affirmative action as a racial preference program. With the "Philadelphia Plan" he launched an era of racial set-sides in government contracts and racial preferences in hiring and college admissions that resulted in an even more massive transfer of wealth to blacks.[239] Even though racial preferences violated the fundamental principle of neutral standards that had just been won by the civil rights movement, the Supreme Court defended them, when they were challenged at the end of the decade, as reparations for past injustices: "Government may take race into account," wrote Justice Brennan, " . . . to remedy disadvantages cast on minorities by past racial prejudice."[240] In a concurring opinion, Justice Thurgood Marshall justified racial preferences as an effort to "remedy the effects of . . . centuries of unequal treatment."[241]

Robinson dismisses this entire history—and the untold millions spent on affirmative action—with a sneer of contempt: "America followed slavery with more than a hundred combined years of legal racial segregation and

236. The figure was calculated for this text by Robert Rector of the Heritage Foundation.
237. Robert Rector and William F. Lauber, *America's Failed $5.4 Trillion War on Poverty* (Heritage Foundation, 1995).
238. Thernstrom, *America in Black and White*, pp. 172–73.
239. And, ironically, slowed the progress of black advancement. Ibid.
240. Ibid., p. 415.
241. Ibid., p. 417. Under pressure from the political left, other groups—women in particular—became beneficiaries of these programs. This has prompted many critics of my ad to claim that the programs cannot be regarded as a form of reparations. This objection is completely illogical, however, tantamount to claiming that one can only have a privilege or a right if it is exclusive.

legal racial discrimination of one variety or another.... The country then began to rub itself with the memory-emptying salve of contemporaneousness. If the wrong did not just occur, it did not occur at all in a way that would render the living responsible."[242]

This denial of the American conscience—and of its manifest deeds— is integral to the reparations claimants' portrait of America as an embodiment of racial evil. "America is one of the cruelest nations in the world when it comes to black folk," declared Chicago Alderman Dorothy Tillman before a large audience of University of Chicago students and faculty. She had been invited to the university by the campus left to prep them for an appearance I was scheduled to make a few days later. It did not occur to Tillman or her audience that American blacks are not noticeably fleeing a country that is so cruel to them; or that the Immigration and Naturalization Service has to turn away thousands of refugees from black countries—like Haiti, Ethiopia, Somalia, Rwanda and the Congo—who are seeking a safe haven in America because of the cruelty of *their* governments. Continuing her crude attack, Tillman said: "America owes us a debt and we intend to collect. The white ruling class accumulated enormous wealth from slavery, either directly or indirectly. Virtually every white person in America reaped some benefits by either owning slaves, investing in the slave industry, or purchasing slave produced products. Meanwhile, blacks received absolutely nothing."[243]

This preposterous claim can be put alongside Robinson's equally absurd statement that the economic gap between whites and blacks "has been static since the Emancipation Proclamation."[244] The record says just the opposite. In the years between 1940 and 1995, for example, the median income of black males rose from 41 percent to 67 percent that of white

242. Robinson, *The Debt,* p. 230.
243. Vanessa Cordonnier, "Local Groups Plan to Protest Horowitz Visit," *Chicago Maroon,* 8 May 2001.
244. Randall Robinson, Transafrica Forum transcript, www.transafricaforum.org/reports/print/reparations_print.shtml. In the last decade, a tendentious literature has appeared attempting to prove the thesis: "The notion embodied in the 'sedimentation of racial inequality' is that in central ways the cumulative effects of the past have seemingly cemented blacks to the bottom of society's economic hierarchy." Melvin L. Oliver and Thomas M. Shapiro, *Black Wealth, White Wealth: A New Perspective on Racial Inequality* (New York, 1997), p. 5. Cf. Claud Anderson, *Black Labor, White Wealth: The Search for Power and Economic Justice* (Bethesda, 1994). The Oliver/Shapiro study is far more substantial, but both arguments treat blacks largely as the objects of impersonal forces, and fail to confront the success of other highly discriminated against and impoverished groups like Jews and Asians, not to mention West Indian born or descended blacks who perform at the American mean.

males, while black females' median income rose from 36 percent to 87 percent of that of white females. [245] In the same period, the percentage of black families with income below the poverty line declined from 87 percent to 26 percent.[246] The percentage of black males in middle-class occupations has increased *six times* in fifty years (from 5.2 percent in 1940 to 32 percent in 1990); for black females it has increased *nine times* over the same period (from 6.4 percent in 1940 to 58.9 percent in 1990).[247]

As a result of these gains, 50 percent of black families are now solidly middle class (as compared to only 1 percent in 1940) along with the vast majority of American families of all ethnicities and colors.[248] In 1994, black household earnings exceeded that of whites in 130 cities and counties across the nation.[249]

It is also true, of course, that despite these dramatic changes, poverty persists among too many blacks—some 26 percent of the black population, as already noted. This poverty has been thoroughly analyzed, however, and has been shown to result from factors that are not determined by racial barriers. For example, poverty was once the result of low-paying jobs, and black poverty was powerfully affected by job discrimination. By the end of the twentieth century, however, discrimination had been outlawed for decades. In contemporary America, poverty for all racial groups is almost entirely the result of failure to work. In 1995, only 2.5 percent of black men who were fully employed had incomes below the poverty line.[250]

It is a well-established fact that the black poverty gap is greatly impacted by astronomical out-of-wedlock birthrates of black Americans: 83 percent of black children who are poor have been born out of wedlock and are being raised in homes with no fathers.[251] A child raised in a single-parent, female-headed household is five times more likely to be poor—regardless of race or ethnic background—than a child raised in a two-parent family. This cannot be attributed to slavery (as it often is) because it is a recent phenomenon, postdating the end of slavery by more than a

---

245. Ibid., p. 195. Also, McWhorter, *Losing the Race*.
246. Thernstrom, *America in Black and White*, p. 233.
247. Ibid., p. 185.
248. *Poverty in the United States: 1995* (Washington, D.C.: U.S. Government Printing Office, 1996). The Thernstroms define "middle-class" as twice the income of the poverty level.
249. John McWhorter, "What's Holding Blacks Back?" *City Journal*, April 2001.
250. *Poverty in the United States: 1995*, table 3. Thernstrom, *America in Black and White*, p. 242.
251. Irwin Garfinkel and Sara McLanahan, *Single Mothers and Their Children* (Lanham, Md., 1986), pp. xix, 14–15, 30.

hundred years.[252] As late as 1960, two-thirds of all black children were born into two-parent families. Fifty years later, two-thirds of black children are born out of wedlock.[253]

"It is family structure that largely divides the haves from the have-nots in the black community," conclude Stephan and Abigail Thernstrom in their path-breaking study, *America in Black and White*. "The population in poverty is made up overwhelmingly of single mothers."[254] The broken family structure of the black community dates from the 1960s and the inception of government welfare programs which have dramatically and adversely affected black families in particular. There is no obvious connection between *these* facts and slavery, or between these facts and *de jure* or *de facto* discrimination; and no proponent of reparations has made any attempt to establish one.

The claim that *de jure* and *de facto* discrimination are responsible for the significant achievement gaps between blacks and other ethnic groups is a claim of ideology, not science. It is based on a Marxist race model that divides society into race victimizers and race victims. In this model, the accountable individual disappears into the group, and the members of victim groups are regarded as lacking either the free will or the ability to function as subjects. They are perceived, instead, as the objects of historical forces over which they can have no control. This is a social elitism that denies the equal humanity of those it labels victims. But if three-quarters of all black families in America have managed to raise themselves above the poverty line, then what has prevented the other quarter from doing the same?[255] The answer certainly can't be racism, because all the parties in question are black.

Given the dramatic trends of black upward mobility in the last sixty years, it is far more reasonable to assume that if there *are* lingering legacies of slavery, segregation and discrimination they are rapidly vanishing, than to conclude that their accelerating damage is so great that reparations

---

252. Even the destruction of the black family in slavery has been significantly exaggerated in the rhetoric of the left. Cf. "The Myth of the Absent Family," in Eugene Genovese, *Roll Jordan Roll: The World the Slaves Made* (New York, 1976), pp. 450 et seq. "Slaves created impressive norms of family life, including as much of a nuclear family norm as conditions permitted, and . . . they entered the postwar social system with a remarkably stable base." Fogel, *Without Contract or Consent*, p. 165, and Gutman, *Been in the Storm So Long*.

253. Thernstrom, *America in Black and White*, p. 240.

254. Ibid., p. 237.

255. Cf. Robinson, n. 233 above.

are required to overcome them. It is certainly not clear that all or even a majority of blacks alive today suffer economic injuries from past injustice requiring reparative measures, and it is an unanswered question as to whether those blacks who are still poor are suffering from the legacies of oppression or from personal dysfunctions which have little to do with "social injustice" or race.

■ ■

The presentation of the reparations claim as an economic demand is itself misplaced. It diminishes and obscures the moral dimensions of the slavery issue. Slavery, as James Madison said, is "the most oppressive dominion of man over man,"[256] and as such is an offense to the human spirit. But instead of focusing on *this* fact, reparations advocates treat slavery as a form of theft and urge their constituencies to line up for an overdue pay day. After the Chicago City Council vote overwhelmingly in favor of reparations, Dorothy Tillman said: "America owes blacks a debt because when we built this country on free labor... wealth was handed down to the white community."[257]

But as already noted, the slave plantations were destroyed, the individual wealth from slavery largely confiscated and used to pay off the costs of the war to end it. Moreover, the alleged contribution of the slave economy to ("white") American wealth has been greatly exaggerated. The claim that the slave system played a key role in the industrialization of the American economy, for example, is intellectually respectable, but it is also speculative and contested. During the era of slavery, contemporary observers regularly noted the economic backwardness of the South, compared with the industrial development of the North. To this day, the question of whether the slave economy was a drag on the southern economy is a point of historical contention. The post-slavery South has long been the poorest region of the United States. The subject of whether the slave economy was a net asset to the national economy as a whole is the center of an ongoing dispute among economic historians, which has not been resolved after a century and a half of debate.[258]

---

256. Thomas G. West, *Vindicating the Founders* (New York, 1977), p. 5.
257. Gary Washburn, "Daley, Council Join in Slavery Apology," *Chicago Tribune*, 18 May 2000.
258. Mark M. Smith, *Debating Slavery: Economy and Society in the Antebellum American South* (Cambridge, 1988), ch. 6, "The Profitability of Slavery as a System." Cf. Robert Fogel and Stanley Engermann, *Time on the Cross: The Economics of American Negro Slavery* (New York, 1974), pp. 59 et seq.

If looked at from the perspective of the slaves themselves, the economic argument for reparations does not become much stronger. The claim that all of a slave's labor was "free labor" is a simple misunderstanding of economic realities. During the nineteenth century, most work—even of the labor force that was free—was subsistence labor. Almost the entire income of a nineteenth-century worker was spent in keeping himself and his family sheltered and alive. Slaves were housed, clothed and fed by their owners. Since owners viewed their slaves as capital, they had a vested interest in their health and well-being, and not in keeping them in the concentration camps fantasized by reparations advocates. Consequently, the diet and shelter of slaves were often comparable to those of the free labor force.[259] Because of the costs of this upkeep, owners did not begin to make a profit from the labor of an individual slave until he or she reached twenty-six years of age.[260] According to the calculations of Fogel and Engermann, over a slave's lifetime the amount of wealth the owner was able to appropriate from his or her labor (i.e., the amount of labor that was actually unpaid) was approximately 12 percent of the income the slave earned.[261] This is far less than the free labor that is currently expropriated by the federal government in the form of income taxes from the average U.S. citizen.[262] The relatively small percentage of actually expropriated slave income does not make slavery less repellent or the expropriation more acceptable; it merely serves to put the claim for the return of "stolen" wealth in perspective.

An equally problematic issue for the reparations claim is the current economic prosperity of blacks in America, relative to that of black people anywhere else. The average income of a black person in America is twenty to fifty times the income of the contemporary inhabitants of the West African nations from which the slaves were taken. The average income in Benin, one of the principal slave trading states, for example, is $380.[263]

---

259. Fogel and Engermann, *Time on the Cross,* pp. 109 et seq.
260. Ibid., p. 153: "Prior to age 26, the accumulated expenditures by planters on slaves were greater than the average accumulated income which they took from them."
261. Ibid. Fogel and Engermann also showed that a significant number of planters actually developed forms of reward, profit sharing and payment for their slaves, pp. 144 et seq.
262. Including the taxes that funded the net transfer of approximately $1.5 trillion in welfare funds to African-Americans in the last 35 years. According to statistics released by Americans for Tax Reform, the average American citizen is forced to work 187 uncompensated days a year to pay for government. Press release, July 6, 2001.
263. According to the Census Bureau, per capita income among blacks in the U.S. in 1999 was $14,397. *Money Income in the United States* (Washington: U.S. Census Bureau, 2000), p. viii.

This does not even take into consideration the social environment, the insecurity of life generally in Africa, the political instability, and the prevalence of epidemics—factors that have kept to an absolute minimum any migration of African-Americans to Africa. "Does anyone seriously suggest that blacks in America today would be better off if they were in Africa?" asks the African-American economist Thomas Sowell, putting a bottom line on the issue. "If not, then what is the compensation for?"[264]

■ ■

There is a racial aspect to the reparations claim, which both proponents and critics have been reluctant to confront. It is reflected in the subtitle of Robinson's book, "What America Owes to Blacks," and in the determined reference of reparations partisans to "246 years of slavery" as the baseline for their grievance against the government of the United States. That government was established in 1776 with the signing of the Declaration of Independence. It was thus in existence for less than ninety years before the Thirteenth Amendment outlawed slavery. Robinson knows this but, like every other reparations advocate, chooses to ignore it. What could possibly be the motivation behind a sleight of hand that makes America responsible for England's crimes, if not a determination to subordinate every other historical factor to race?

This is also the only possible inference of the following sentence taken from *The Debt*: "Well before the birth of our country, Europe and the eventual United States [*sic*] perpetrated a heinous wrong against the peoples of Africa—and sustained and benefited from the wrong for centuries."[265]

It is a striking fact that no American Indian nations are indicted in *The Debt* or are named in any of the reparations claims made on behalf of American blacks. The historical record shows that Choctaws, Chicasaws, Cherokees, Creeks and Seminoles owned black slaves and that black slavery persisted among them until after the Civil War, when the United States government through a formal treaty forced the tribes to end the practice.[266] What can explain this omission from the reparations indictment except that the debt of slavery per se is less an issue for its proponents than the imagined debt of race? An African-American critic of reparations, Adolph Reed, concludes just that: "The deeper appeal of reparations

264. "Reparations for Slavery," Creators Syndicate, 14 July 2000.
265. Robinson, *The Debt*, p. 230.
266. Dinesh D'Souza, *The End of Racism* (New York, 1995), p. 75; Theda Perdue, *Slavery and the Evolution of Cherokee Society* (Tennessee, 1988), pp. 38–39.

talk for its proponents is to create or stress a sense of racial people-hood as the primary basis for political identity."[267]

The racial perspective of the reparations movement can be seen even more clearly in the claims advanced by African nations themselves. These claims are supported by the reparations movement in the United States.[268] While African nations clamor for reparations from the western nations, which abolished slavery more than a century ago, there are still tens and perhaps hundreds of thousands of slaves in the African nations—the Sudan, Ghana, Mauritania, Benin, Gabon, Mali and the Ivory Coast.[269] By making no claims against African governments that participated in the slave trade (and still do) reparations proponents make clear that their grievance is not against an institution—slavery—and those who benefited from it; but that slavery is a means for them to formulate an indictment against Europeans and their descendants—in a word, against whites.

Even as the efforts of Americans to abolish slavery are ignored or discounted, so is the fact that the suppression of the African slave trade was the work of the colonial powers that accomplished the emancipation of African slaves against great resistance from the Africans themselves. Slavery not only flourished in Africa after the American Civil War, it greatly increased, since slaves became cheaper when Caribbean and South American markets were closed. It was the actions of the European colonial powers that gradually eliminated most vestiges of slavery from the African continent. British abolitionists in particular "forced antislavery treaties on hundreds of remote rulers, blockaded distant ports and rivers, boarded foreign ships at risk of war, bribed oriental chiefs and sultans, spent billions in today's currencies, years on monotonous patrols and died in the thousands of malaria and yellow fever" to suppress the trade. British and American gunboats destroyed the slave ports on Africa's western coast. When the trade was finally suppressed in 1808, rioters protested in the Gold Coast (now Ghana), and the King of Bonny (now Nigeria) told the British: "Your country, however great, can never stop a trade ordained by God himself."[270] The present reparations movement in Africa—fully

267. Adolph Reed, "The Case Against Reparations," *The Progressive,* December 2000. Reed refers to the claims advanced by the campaign as "racially defined reparations."
268. "And then, of course, there are the billions of dollars owed to Africa and the descendants of slaves for wealth lost in a post-slavery environment of government-approved discrimination." Robinson, *The Debt,* p. 244.
269. Jeffrey White, "Africans Undermine Reparations Claims," *National Post,* 21 April 2001.
270. Ibid.

supported by its American counterparts—is thus directed at the very parties who righted the wrong, and did not institute it in the first place.

As noted earlier, in defending this double standard reparations advocates employ an argument similar to the academic left's claim that only
whites can be racists (because "only whites have power"). They argue
incoherently that African slavery was not really slavery; or, if it was slavery, it was not really bad. Thus Robinson: "While King Affonso [of Kongo]
was no stranger to slavery, which was practiced throughout most of the
known world, he had understood slavery as a condition befalling prison-
ers of war, criminals, and debtors, out of which slaves could earn, or even
marry, their way. This was nothing like seeing this wholly new and brutal commercial practice of slavery where tens of thousands of his subjects
were dragged off in chains."[271] Dorothy Benton-Lewis also argues that
only American slavers were racist or brutal: "It is American slavery that
put a color on slavery. And American slavery is not like the slavery of
Africa and ancient times. This was dehumanizing, brutal and barbaric
slavery that subjugated people and turned them into a profit."[272]

Both claims are false, and based on casuistry. A leading academic
expert on slavery, Orlando Patterson, who studied fifty-five slave societies,
writes:

> It has often been remarked that slavery in the Americas is unique in
> the primary role of race as a factor in determining the condition and
> treatment of slaves. *This statement betrays an appalling ignorance of
> the comparative data on slave societies....* Throughout the Islamic
> world, for instance, race was a vital issue. The light-skinned Tuareg
> and related groups had decidedly racist attitudes toward the Negroes
> they conquered. Throughout the Islamic empires, European and Turk-
> ish slaves were treated quite differently from slaves south of the Sahara
> Desert.... Slavery [in Africa] was more than simply "subordination";
> it was considered a degraded condition, reinforced by racist attitudes
> among the Arab slave owners.[273] [emphasis added]

The idea that African slavery was not "commercial" and therefore
benign is an invention of the reparations proponents. No ownership of
human beings is benign. The claim is based on the fact that some slave
practices and some slave masters made life less onerous for their human

271. Robinson, *The Debt*, p. 26.
272. MIT debate, http://video.C-span.org:8080/ramgen/ndrive/e040701_slavery.rm.
273. Orlando Patterson, *Slavery and Social Death: A Comparative Study* (Harvard,
    1982), pp. 176, 193.

chattel. But this was true in America as well. Moreover, plantation slavery, which reparations proponents regard as especially exploitative, was widespread in Africa: "In the nineteenth century, slaves on the East African coast became enmeshed in a developing plantation economy that in many ways resembled the plantation economies of the Western Hemisphere. Plantations were large-scale, specialized units that developed in order to serve the needs of a vast and widespread market for particular commodities."[274] Writing of African slavery before 1600, the historian Paul Lovejoy notes: "For those who were enslaved, the dangers involved forced marches, inadequate food, sexual abuse, and death on the road."[275] Slaves in Africa were used for mining gold and salt, and for ritual sacrifices. Families were separated. Men were executed to make their women available for concubinage. Young males were castrated for court use and "death from unsuccessful operations could be as large as nine boys out of ten."[276]

This information is readily available to Randall Robinson and other reparations proponents. But they have chosen to ignore the historical reality in order to prosecute their cause, which has much to do with anger and little to do with justice.

Black novelist Zora Neale Hurston had a different response to African slavery: "The white people held my people in slavery here in America. They bought us, it is true, and exploited us. But the inescapable fact that stuck in my craw was [that] my people had sold me.... My own people had exterminated whole nations and torn families apart for profit before the strangers got their chance at a cut. It was a sobering thought. It impressed upon me the universal nature of greed and glory."[277] It was this kind of universal outlook that inspired Americans from the beginning to enlarge their humanity and finally embrace the equality of all. The reparations movement is an attempt to take a giant step backwards from this humanistic perspective which Hurston expresses so well.

---

274. Frederick Cooper, *Plantation Slavery on the East Coast of Africa* (Portsmouth, 1997), p. 3.
275. Lovejoy, *Transformations in Slavery*, p. 35.
276. Ibid. Writing of gold mining in the period 1600–1800 Lovejoy observes: "The practice of using slaves in gold production continued under Asante. The risk of death in the pits was considerable because of the environment and relatively low level of technology. The rainy season left the ground damp for months, thereby increasing the danger of cave-in. This risk was perhaps a major reason why custom forbade the Akan from mining gold themselves." Roger Morton, who studied Arab slavery in Kenya, says: "Rendered inferior by birth, occupation, and color, slaves became natural objects of abuse for the Muslim free-born." Cited by Patterson, *Slavery and Social Death*.
277. Zora Neale Hurston, *Dust Tracks on a Road* (New York, 1991), p. 145, cited in D'Souza, *The End of Racism*, p. 74.

■ ■

Americans generally do not think of themselves as racists or oppressors, and there is no reason they should. America was a pioneer in the fight against slavery, and in establishing the first multiracial society in human history. During the last half-century Americans have voted equal rights to African-American citizens and supported massive compensations to African-Americans and others who have lagged behind. To be indicted after such efforts, and in these unrelenting terms, is offensive and insulting. The political logic of the reparations claim itself defies reason. It is not feasible to convince people who have good reason to regard themselves as compassionate fellow citizens to think of themselves as oppressors instead. Nor will one persuade them to vote damages for injuries they have not inflicted.

The reparations claim is a hostile assault on America and its history. Its divisive message and fallacious views can only have a profoundly adverse effect on those who embrace it, making it impossible for them to see their own past clearly, or to find a way to an American future. Keith Richburg spent three years as a *Washington Post* reporter in Africa and came back with this self-understanding: "By an accident of birth, I am a black man born in America, and everything I am today—my culture and attitudes, my sensibilities, loves, and desires—derives from that one simple and irrefutable truth."[278] If the negative claims of the reparations argument were true, black Americans would have no usable American past; no element of the national heritage would be available to them; they would have no reason to feel American in their soul. It is a short step from the reparations argument to the separatist idea that black Americans have no home in this country, and indeed this threat is just beneath the surface of Randall Robinson's text: "Until America's white ruling class accepts the fact that the book never closes on massive un-redressed social wrongs, America can have no future as one people."[279]

Thomas Sowell asks the following question in connection with the reparations claim: "Is anyone made better off by being supplied with resentments and distractions from the task of developing the capabilities that pay off in a booming economy and a high-tech world? Whites may experience a passing annoyance over the reparations issue, but blacks—especially young blacks—can sustain more lasting damage from misallocating their time, attention and efforts."[280] I was made painfully aware of

278. Keith B. Richburg, *Out of America: A Black Man Confronts Africa* (New York, 1998), p. 248.
279. Robinson, *The Debt*, p. 208.
280. Sowell, "Reparations for Slavery," 14 July 2000.

these negative impacts in my encounters with black students at the colleges I visited. Many of their attitudes were expressed in a letter written to the editor of *The Lariat,* the student paper at Baylor University. The writer was a young woman who wanted to complain about my reparations ad: "My ancestors provided this nation with more than 200 years of hard, free labor and instead of their 40 acres and a mule, what did they get? Nothing. Nothing but more than 100 more years of hate, Black Codes, Jim Crow laws, the KKK, lynchings, segregation, miscegenation [*sic*], oppression, poverty, fear and more hate."[281]

This young woman was attending a university whose tuition and board was $20,000 a year, yet she was filled with such resentment and feelings of futility and victimization that she could not appreciate the fact that all her ancestors really received for their suffering were the opportunities she had been given. Her ancestors had not been requited in their own lives and no longer could be. Her life, on the other hand, was before her, and as their descendant she had miraculous blessings to count. But in her anger, she could see none.

The difficulty I had in making this argument to most of the black students who attended my appearances revealed how effective the suppression of ideas has become at the educational institutions that are shaping their futures. For observing that white Americans died to free America's slaves and to suggest that a bond between them was created in this sacrifice, I was tarred a "racist." For praising Jefferson and Lincoln as heroes of liberty for *all* Americans, I was condemned as "anti-black." For arguing that America's promise can be real for everyone who embraces it, I was dismissed as "insensitive" to the descendants of slaves.

In contrast to my opponents, whose passions *are* disturbingly focused on race, I am convinced that the fault-line in American society is not racial but political, that the great obstacle to a constructive approach on these issues is an agenda that is hostile to American democracy, and that the partisans of this agenda have no hesitancy in using "race" as a political weapon. Fortunately, there is in fact a bond forged out of this nation's heritage that does stretch across the racial and political spectrum. I also had defenders everywhere, of all races, and among them those who did not share my specific views, but believed in the importance of engaging them with respect.

This manuscript was completed, appropriately enough, on the Fourth of July. On that day ceremonial tributes to the Fourth were published in

---

281. Pamela A. Hairston, letter to the editor of the *Baylor Lariat* ("Reparations fair, necessary response to injustices caused by Black Codes"), 20 March 2001.

newspaper columns across the country. Two of them that came to my notice as I put this work aside were from the other side of the political spectrum and were written by journalists who were black. The fact that I found myself in wholehearted agreement with both of these writers provides a note of optimism with which to end this story.

The first was written by Clarence Page, whom I have known and respected, but who had penned a harsh (and uncharacteristically unkind) attack on me in the midst of my battles. To commemorate this national day, he wrote about a black state senator from Tennessee who had refused to pay homage to the flag with her colleagues, saying: "I can't pledge allegiance to a flag that represents the former colonies that enslaved our ancestors." In her separatism, the senator was not alone, Page observed. "Many African-Americans feel an odd disconnection around the flag, the Fourth of July and other expressions of patriotism to a country founded in significant part by, oh, yes, slaveholders." But then he said:

> As a fellow descendant of slaves—and an Army veteran—I disagree.... The pledge is not a declaration of existing reality. It is an expression of one's commitment to a goal worth achieving. Sure, this country has yet to achieve perfection in the liberty and justice department, but we're working on it. I see the pledge as a promise to keep working on it. Further, I resent the implication that patriotism cannot really be, to coin a popular implication-loaded phrase, "a black thing." African-Americans have fought and sacrificed themselves in every American war—even under the command of that slaveholder George Washington. If anybody has reason to be patriotic, it is us.... The genius of our slaveholding Founders... was in their having the foresight to create documents that had better values than those they practiced.... They... set up a challenge for the people of this nation to never shirk from the task of making liberty and justice a reality for everybody. A flag that stands for those values is worth pledging allegiance to.[282]

In his column Page also mentioned a newly published book, which was written by a veteran civil rights activist and journalist, Roger Wilkins. It was called *Jefferson's Pillow: The Founding Fathers and the Dilemma of Black Patriotism.* Wilkins' uncle Roy had been head of the NAACP in the golden era of civil rights struggle, and like others of his generation, the nephew had veered to the left in the years that followed. Previously, Roger Wilkins was always associated in my mind with a bottomless scowl as he talked about race in television interviews and newspaper columns.

---

282. Clarence Page, "Can Blacks Be Patriotic? Should They Be?" *Chicago Tribune,* 5 July 2001.

I vividly remember his comments on some anniversary of the civil rights struggles—perhaps it was in 1993, thirty years after Martin Luther King had his famous dream of a color-blind American future. Wilkins' brow furrowed and his expression grew dark as he said how little had changed for black people in America, and how dire were the prospects they faced. His pessimism caused me to wonder, then, about that American future of which King had dreamed. But on July 4, 2001, Roger Wilkins' views had undergone a dramatic change—or so it seemed to me.

His column appeared in the *New York Times* and was taken from the final pages of his new book. It was titled "Black Patriotism Enlarges the American Tradition."[283] It began: "One famous African-American has been quoted recently as saying, 'At no time have I ever felt like an American.' Well, I have—all my life. . . .

> The privilege of defining me rests with my African ancestors, who had the fortitude to survive the Middle Passage and the "seasoning" meted out by their American jailers. It rests with those enlightened philosophers who inserted the idea of human equality into the ideology of the West—including the founders of America, notably Thomas Jefferson, the quintessential man of ambiguity. . . . I have seen and participated in a remarkable enlargement of American opportunity and justice. From the one-room segregated schoolhouse in Missouri where I started school through a lifelong friendship with [Supreme Court Justice] Thurgood Marshall and a rich variety of struggles for justice, I have had the fortune to participate in an astonishing American effort to adjust life, as it is lived, to the ideals proclaimed by the founders. While the transformation is far from complete, the change has nevertheless been so dramatic that my belief in American possibilities remains profound.

There was hard-won wisdom in the words of Page and Wilkins. Theirs were testaments to the resilience of the American dream, and reassuring coming from descendants of slaves and critics of American life. They reaffirmed the possibility that the American Founders did create a crucible so powerful in its principles that it could—out of the multiracial, multiethnic variety of our remarkable people—finally make them one.

---

283. *New York Times*, 4 July 2001.

Acknowledgments

I want to thank Scott Rubush and Jennifer Kabbany for helping me with research and fact-checking; Monty Warner, J. P. Duberg, Bruce Donaldson and Stephen Brooks for orchestrating my media and campus campaigns; Terry Brown and Eric Fitzgerald for looking after me on my tour; Richard Poe for his counsel; John Campbell, and my office staff for their support; and Peter for being a writer's editor.

I also want to thank my wife, April, and my stepson, Jon, for making my home a joy to work and live in.

INDEX